CAMBRIDGE
Lower Secondary English

Lucy Birchenough, Clare Constant, Naomi Hursthouse, Ian Kirby, Nikki Smith

Series Editors: Julia Burchell and Mike Gould

Stage 7: Student's Book

William Collins' dream of knowledge for all began with the publication of his first book in 1819. A self-educated mill worker, he not only enriched millions of lives, but also founded a flourishing publishing house. Today, staying true to this spirit, Collins books are packed with inspiration, innovation and practical expertise. They place you at the centre of a world of possibility and give you exactly what you need to explore it.

HarperCollins Publishers Ltd
The News Building
1 London Bridge Street
London SE1 9GF

First edition 2015

10 9 8 7 6 5 4 3

ISBN 978-0-00-811690-3

www.collins.co.uk

A catalogue record for this book is available from the British Library.

Printed in Italy by Grafica Veneta

All exam-style questions and sample answers in this student book are written by the authors.

Authors: Julia Burchell and Mike Gould
Commissioning Editor: Ben Pettitt and Cathy Martin
Development Editor: Lucy Hobbs
Managing Editor: Sarah Thomas
Copy Editor: Sonya Newland
Proofreader: Ros Davies
Typesetter: Jouve India Private Ltd
Cover design: Lucy Harvey at ink-tank and associates ltd

Contents

Chapter 6 • Writing to analyse and compare

Chapter 7 • Testing your skills

Introduction

The Collins Cambridge Lower Secondary English Student's Book offers a unique skills-building approach to the Cambridge Lower Secondary English curriculum framework, Stage 7.

It is divided into seven chapters. Each of the first six chapters focuses on a different writing 'purpose', whilst the seventh offers the chance to put all the skills into practice through exam-style tasks.

The first six chapters address these purposes:

- Writing to explore and reflect
- Writing to inform and explain
- Writing to argue and persuade
- Descriptive writing
- Narrative writing
- Writing to analyse and compare

Each of these six chapters is based loosely on a theme such as 'animal rights' or 'natural mysteries' and enables you to learn and practise a range of general reading, writing, speaking and listening skills, in particular those which are part of writing for the specific purpose which is featured. You will read a wide variety of texts from writers from many social, cultural and historical backgrounds and will write a wide range of texts yourself. Each chapter provides you with opportunities to complete two substantial tasks to show what you have achieved: one on Reading and responding to texts, and one on Writing for each particular type or purpose. From these you will be able to assess your work to see how your abilities are developing.

The book has also been designed so that you re-visit particularly important skills several times across the chapters. In some cases this is to make sure that you can apply the skills in new contexts and in others it will be because a new aspect of the skill has been introduced to help you to progress.

Key features of the book include 'Check your progress' panels at the end of each two or four page unit. These will help you assess your own progress. Watch out for these.

Three other text features to note are 'Checklist for success' which lists criteria to cover when completing a task, 'Key terms' which define important literary and language terms and 'Vocabulary' panels to support you when reading an extract.

Chapter 7 offers you the chance to show what you have learnt during this stage and encourages you to assess your work to gain an understanding of how errors can occur.

We hope our skills-building approach helps you and your teachers to fulfil the demands of your English Course in an enjoyable and engaging way.

Julia Burchell

Mike Gould

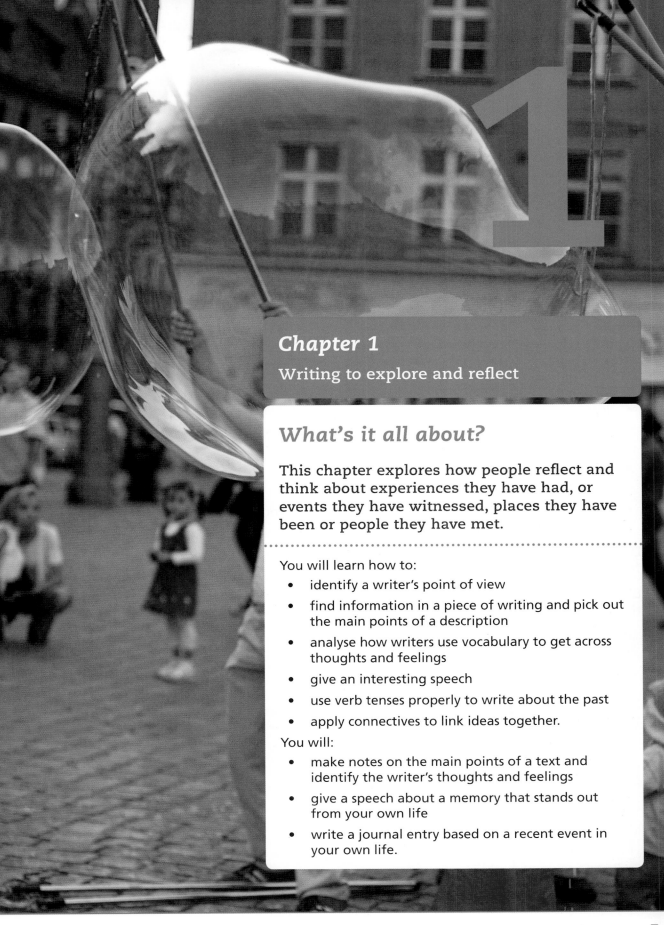

Chapter 1
Writing to explore and reflect

What's it all about?

This chapter explores how people reflect and think about experiences they have had, or events they have witnessed, places they have been or people they have met.

You will learn how to:
- identify a writer's point of view
- find information in a piece of writing and pick out the main points of a description
- analyse how writers use vocabulary to get across thoughts and feelings
- give an interesting speech
- use verb tenses properly to write about the past
- apply connectives to link ideas together.

You will:
- make notes on the main points of a text and identify the writer's thoughts and feelings
- give a speech about a memory that stands out from your own life
- write a journal entry based on a recent event in your own life.

What is writing to explore and reflect?

You will learn how to:
- identify the main types of personal writing
- plan to write personally.

Writing to explore and reflect is usually personal writing, focusing on the experiences, thoughts and feelings of a specific person. Personal writing is considered to be non-fiction, as it is based on true events. It may be written in a **narrative** style to engage the reader, but it will also include **non-narrative** features such as lists of dates and real events.

Introducing the skills

People write personal accounts for many reasons – to share their life stories, to reveal the truth or to express their feelings. There are different types of personal writing. For example:

- **diary:** a daily account of events and actions

- **journal:** an ongoing account of thoughts and feelings, possibly in response to particular events; it does not have to be written every day

- **biography:** the story of someone's life, written by someone else.

- **autobiography:** the story of someone's life, written by themselves.

Diaries and journals focus on the events, thoughts or feelings of life *as it is carrying on now*.

Biographies and autobiographies focus on the events, thoughts and feelings of life *in the past*.

Key terms

narrative: a series of connected events presented in the form of a story (fiction or non-fiction); a narrative usually has at least one main character and often includes their thoughts and feelings

non-narrative: information (usually non-fiction) that is presented in factual or statistical groups, not necessarily in chronological order (e.g. in a leaflet, dictionary or encyclopedia)

1 Look at these starter sentences. Copy the grid below and complete the second column with the type of personal writing you think each one is.

Starter sentence	Type of personal writing
Today we went to the zoo.	diary
I am feeling a bit sad at the moment.	
William Shakespeare lived for 52 years.	
My life has been both strange and wonderful.	
It is cold outside today.	

Anybody can write a diary or journal, and people often keep them private. Biographies and autobiographies are usually written about famous people, and they are published for others to read.

2 Look at the following titles of biographies and autobiographies. For each one, write down why you think it was written or what it is about.

a) *Faster than Lightning* – Usain Bolt

b) *Dreams from My Father* – Barack Obama

c) *Boy* – Roald Dahl

d) *Teacher Man* – Frank McCourt

e) *Unbroken* – Laura Hillenbrand

3 Complete a grid like the one below, adding events and feelings from your own life.

Diary (today's events)	Journal (current feelings)	Biography (information about other people)	Autobiography (information about yourself)
went to the zoo	annoyed (sister won't share bike)	best friend was school swimming champion	broke my arm when seven

Applying the skills

4 Choose one type of personal writing from the grid in Question 3 and write a full paragraph about yourself.

Check your progress:

I can identify types of personal writing.

I can identify the purposes of different types of personal writing.

I can identify suitable ideas for my own personal writing.

Extracting information from personal writing

You will learn how to:
- identify a writer's overall point of view (big idea)
- select the key parts of the writing (small points).

When you read reflective writing, it is important to understand what the writer is trying to tell you. Writers usually have one *big idea*, which is made up of many *small points* linked together.

Introducing the skills

Read this description from an autobiography. In it, a young boy is describing an adult he knows.

> But by far the most **loathsome** thing about Mrs Pratchett was the filth that clung around her. Her apron was grey and greasy. Her blouse had bits of breakfast all over it, toast-crumbs and tea stains and splotches of dried egg-yolk. It was her hands, however, that disturbed us the most. They were disgusting. They were black with dirt and grime.
>
> From *Boy* by Roald Dahl

Vocabulary

loathsome: causing hatred or repulsion

1. Are the following statements true or false?
   a) Mrs Pratchett is dirty.
   b) Mrs Pratchett's clothes are covered in the food she ate for lunch.
   c) The worst thing about Mrs Pratchett is her feet.
   d) Mrs Pratchett's apron is green.
   e) It seems like Mrs Pratchett hasn't washed her hands.

2. What is the writer's overall **point of view** about Mrs Pratchett? Choose the most accurate answer.
   a) He enjoys spending time with her.
   b) He does not like her, mostly because of the way she looks.
   c) She is a nice woman even though she is not very clean.

Key terms

point of view: a personal opinion or way of looking at something

A writer's point of view is usually the reason they write something in the first place – it is their 'big idea'.

3 Look at the extract again. Select three pieces of information that helped you decide on the writer's point of view about Mrs Pratchett.

Each piece of information you found is a 'small point'. By looking at lots of small points in a text, you can work out the big idea.

Developing the skills

Even though a writer never says 'In this story, my big idea is…', they sometimes make it easy for you to work it out by giving you clues in the opening sentence.

In the extract from *Boy*, the opening sentence says Mrs Pratchett is 'loathsome'. This gives us a clue that the big idea is that the writer does not like her.

4 Imagine each of the sentences in the grid below is the start of a story. Which words give you a clue about the big idea? Copy and complete the table.

Starter sentence	Clues to the big idea
I always feel grumpy when I am getting ready for school.	'always' and 'grumpy' = the writer doesn't like school
It is wonderful to go to my grandfather's house in Scotland.	
I was ten years old when my life changed forever.	
Exercising is an important part of a healthy lifestyle.	
Although my sister looks like me, we have completely different personalities.	

Although the first sentence of a story might give you a clue to the big idea, you still need to read it all to be sure. You can do this quickly by **skimming** the whole text to understand what the writer is talking about overall.

5 Look at this starter sentence. Find the clues that tell you what this story is going to be about.

> When I was born we were very poor.

6 Now skim through the text to see if you are correct.

> When I was born we were very poor. My father and a friend had founded their first school and we lived in a shabby shack of two rooms opposite the school. I slept with my mother and father in one room and the other was for guests. We had no bathroom or kitchen, and my mother cooked on a wood fire on the ground and washed our clothes at a tap in the school.
>
> From *I am Malala* by Malala Yousafzai

The big idea that the writer wants to tell you about is that her family did not have much money when she was a child.

7 The key word here is 'poor'. Find the small point in the sentence below that links to being poor:

> ...we lived in a shabby shack of two rooms opposite the school.

8 Now **scan** the text for other small points that are linked to being poor. Just choose key words. Copy out the important sections as a bullet-point list or as a spider diagram.

Small point 1: 'shabby shack'

Small point 2:

Small point 3:

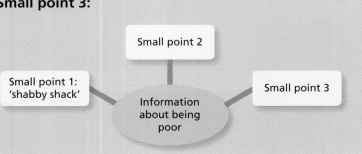

Read the following extract. It is from an autobiography of a young boy who is sent to boarding school.

> Each **dormitory** had about twenty beds in it. These were smallish narrow beds ranged along the walls on either side. Down the centre of the dormitory stood the basins where you washed your hands and face and did your teeth, always with cold water which stood in large jugs on the floor. Once you had entered the dormitory you were not allowed to leave it unless you were reporting to **Matron's** room with some sickness or injury.
>
> From *Boy* by Roald Dahl

Vocabulary

dormitory: a room where lots of people can sleep

Matron: a woman who is in charge

9 Identify the writer's big idea in this extract. Write one sentence to explain it.

10 Create a set of notes to show all the small points that are linked to the big idea.

Checklist for success:

- ✔ Look for key words in the starter sentence to give you clues about the content of the big idea.
- ✔ Use the key words from the big idea to scan the text for your small points.

Check your progress:

I can skim a story to work out the big idea that the writer is trying to tell me.

I can find key words in a starter sentence that give clues about the big idea.

I can scan a story to find small points that link to the big idea.

Understanding writers' language choices

You will learn how to:
- look for clear meanings and hidden meanings in a text
- identify similes and metaphors
- respond, showing understanding of a writer's meaning.

In personal writing, a writer often wishes to present many thoughts and feelings. Some of these will be obvious but others are hidden more deeply. You need to use **inference** or **deduction** to work out what the writer is trying to say.

Introducing the skills

1 Write down five *factual* statements that describe your appearance. For example:

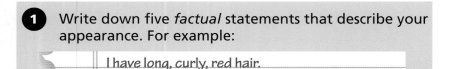

I have long, curly, red hair.

Someone who had never met you would be able to draw a simple picture of you using these statements, because you have described yourself clearly and factually. They would not need to use inference or deduction.

Now read this description. It is from an autobiography of a young girl who has been adopted. She has never met her birth parents and is imagining what her father looks like.

> In my imaginary childish drawing, my birth father is a tall, handsome black man with large hands and dark life lines and a broad smile. He is a rich dark colour, a melting darkness, warm and endless like the dark of sleep. He has broad features, a wide nose, high spread cheeks, wide as the span of a small bird's wing, and a laughing smile.
>
> From *Red Dust Road* by Jackie Kay

Key terms

inference: working out what a writer has suggested by their choice of words (e.g. saying that someone 'drags their feet' suggests that they do not want to go somewhere)

deduction: adding up information in a text to find an overall meaning (e.g. if a student is late for school and has forgotten their books it means they are not very organised)

2 Answer the following questions:

a) What skin colour does Jackie's father have?

b) Is he a small man or a large man? Find two pieces of information.

c) Does he look like he is angry or happy?

Jackie has given several clear pieces of information about how she imagines her birth father looks. This is known as **explicit** meaning. We can also use *inference* to work out what Jackie *feels* about her father. These clues to her feelings are **implicit**.

To work out implicit meaning, you need to look carefully at a writer's words and decide if they suggest something more than their obvious meaning. For example, the word 'rich' suggests that Jackie's father is worth a great deal to her.

Look at the same extract, highlighted to show the words that tell you something directly (explicit) and the words that might have a hidden meaning (implicit). For example, 'melting darkness' implies a comforting feeling that the reader gains from her father's appearance.

> In my imaginary childish drawing, my birth father is a tall, handsome black man with large hands and dark life lines and a broad smile. He is a rich dark colour, a melting darkness, warm and endless like the dark of sleep. He has broad features, a wide nose, high spread cheeks, wide as the span of a small bird's wing, and a laughing smile.
>
> From *Red Dust Road* by Jackie Kay

Key terms

explicit: words that tell the reader something directly

implicit: words that give clues and suggestions to a meaning that the reader must try and work out

3 Copy the final sentence of the extract and highlight the explicit and implicit words.

4 Write a sentence for each implicit word or phrase, explaining what it suggests. Use this starter sentence:

The words...suggest that...

Developing the skills

In the extract, Jackie Kay uses two techniques to develop the implicit meaning – **similes** and **metaphors**.

5 Which of the statements below are similes and which are metaphors? (Tip: one statement contains both.)

a) She is as sweet as sugar.

b) I laughed like a hyena.

c) Usain Bolt is a racing stallion.

d) The afternoon lessons crept by as wearily as a tired tortoise.

e) Daggers of icy steel hung from the ceiling of the cave.

f) Her angry words rolled out like a tsunami of destruction.

g) The morning sun spreads its angelic wings across the land.

h) My karate teacher is a mountain of a man. I feel like a tiny mouse in comparison!

Key terms

simile: a comparison between two things that uses the words 'as' or 'like' (e.g. 'My dad sleeps *like* a bear in hibernation')

metaphor: a type of comparison that describes one thing as if it is something else (e.g. 'In winter, my dad is a bear in hibernation')

6 Choose one of the similes or metaphors in Jackie Kay's description of her father, then write down what it shows the reader. Use this starter sentence:

By using the words…the writer is trying to show us that…

Read the text below. A person is describing the streets where they lived as a young child.

> The road into town was a <u>nightmare of endless vehicles</u>, all <u>jammed together</u> bumper to bumper. The heat was <u>unbearable</u>. It <u>shimmered in waves</u> above the cars and the surface of the road <u>like a hungry eagle</u> waiting to <u>swoop</u> on its <u>prey</u>. Children <u>slumped on back seats</u> and <u>stared longingly</u> at the passers-by on the pavements, as <u>though they had been imprisoned</u> and were <u>waiting to be released</u>.

7 What is the writer trying to tell us about travelling on these streets?

Find a mixture of explicit and implicit words to help you answer the question. Some possible word choices have been underlined for you. The writer has used two similes and one metaphor.

Use the starter sentences in Questions 4 and 6 to help write your answer.

Checklist for success:

✔ Find a mixture of explicit and implicit words to write about in your paragraph.

✔ Identify and explain any similes or metaphors in the passage.

Check your progress:

I can identify similes and metaphors in writing.

I can find explicit and implicit meanings in writing.

I can explain in my own writing the explicit and implicit details a writer uses.

Responding to personal writing

You will learn how to:
- combine the reading skills you have learned when responding to personal writing
- understand what makes a high-level response to personal writing.

Your task

Plan and write two paragraphs about the extract below. You should write:

- one paragraph that explains the big idea and the main points of the story

- one paragraph that explains the writer's thoughts and feelings in the story.

This is the beginning of an autobiography about a boy who moves house at the start of World War I.

> I was set down from the **carrier's** cart at the age of three; and there with a sense of bewilderment and terror my life in the village began. The June grass, amongst which I stood, was taller than I was, and I wept. I had never been so close to grass before. It towered above me and all around me, each blade tattooed with tiger-skins of sunlight. It was knife-edged, dark and a wicked green, thick as a forest and alive with grasshoppers that chirped and chattered and leapt through the air like monkeys. I was lost and didn't know where to move.

Vocabulary

carrier: a person or company that takes goods or people from place to place

A tropic heat oozed up from the ground, rank with sharp odours of roots and nettles. Snow-clouds of elder-blossom banked in the sky, showering upon me the fumes and flakes of their sweet and giddy suffocation. High overhead ran **frenzied** larks, screaming, as though the sky were tearing apart. For the first time in my life I was out of the sight of humans. For the first time in my life I was alone in a world whose behaviour I could neither predict nor fathom: a world of birds that squealed, of plants that stank, of insects that sprang about without warning. I was lost and did not expect to be found again. I put back my head and howled, and the sun hit me smartly on the face, like a bully.

From *Cider with Rosie* by Laurie Lee

Vocabulary

frenzied: wildly excited or uncontrolled

Approaching the task

Before writing your paragraphs, you need to plan for them.

1 What do you think is the *big idea* of this extract? What is the writer trying to tell you overall? Look closely at the opening sentence, then skim the rest of the story for more information.

2 Find five explicit details in the extract – things the writer states directly. Think about the following:

a) where the child is   b) what is going on

c) what he can see or hear.

Create a spider diagram of your ideas:

He is in a village

Explicit details

3 Find five implicit meanings in the extract – things that tell you what the writer is thinking or feeling. Look for similes, metaphors and words with hidden meanings. Write a list of the phrases and what they suggest. For example:

- 'towered above me' suggests that the writer feels tiny compared to the grass
- 'wicked green' suggests...

4 Think of some starter sentences for your paragraphs. For example:

- Paragraph 1: This extract is about...
- Paragraph 2: In this extract, the writer is trying to tell the reader that he felt...
  The words...suggest that...
  The writer implies that...

5 Now write your two paragraphs.

Reflecting on your progress

Response 1

This extract is about a three-year-old boy who does not like the place he is in. He is crying because he has not been in a place like this before, which has tall grass. There are lots of animals like grasshoppers, birds and other insects flying around and making noises. The writer is on his own and it is quite hot in the sun.

Identifies the big idea.

Gives examples of explicit detail.

Shows some implicit understanding.

Comment on Response 1

This response starts well, as the student shows they understand what is going on in the extract. They have picked out some key explicit details, such as that the grass is taller than the boy and that he starts crying. However, the student has only done one part of the task and has not used any words from the text to show what the writer is thinking or feeling.

6 Using the comments above and progress points 1b–3b in the Check your progress section at the end of this chapter, rewrite this response to improve it.

Response 2

This extract is about a small boy who is confused and scared when he arrives in a new place. It is very hot and there are lots of insects and birds flying around. The boy is on his own and does not like the sights and sounds surrounding him. In fact, in this extract the writer is suggesting that all the plants and animals are actually against him. The words 'towered above me' suggest that he feels tiny compared to the grass and as though it is going to attack him. The words 'knife-edged' also suggest that the grass is dangerous. The word 'suffocation' shows us that he is finding it hard to breathe, maybe because he is so scared and is starting to panic. However, when he shows he is upset and starts to 'howl', the sun also gangs up on him by shining its hot rays in his face.

Focuses on feelings.

Highlights implicit meanings.

Personal response shows developed understanding of hidden meanings.

Comment on Response 2

This response shows an understanding of both explicit information and implicit meanings in the text. The student uses the starter sentences to help show what the writer may be feeling, and includes some of the words of the text to prove this.

7 Using the comments above and progress points 1c–3c in the Check your progress section at the end of this chapter, rewrite this response to improve it.

Controlling language in a presentation

You will learn how to:
- write a short anecdote about yourself to use in an informal presentation
- deliver an engaging presentation to an audience
- discuss the effects of your presentation.

A successful presentation keeps an audience engaged through both its written content and its spoken **delivery**.

Introducing the skills

1 Think of the most interesting and the most boring people you know. Make a list of reasons why you like or don't like listening to them talk. Think about *what they say* and *how they say it*.

Read the **anecdote** below from Usain Bolt's autobiography. It describes how he felt when he won his first race as a child.

> *Bang!* Winning was like an explosion, a rush. Joy, freedom, fun – it all hit me at once. Taking the line first felt great, especially in something as big as a school sports day race, an event that officially made me the fastest kid in Waldensia!
>
> From *Faster than Lightning* by Usain Bolt

2 Usain Bolt's main idea in this anecdote is to show how thrilled he was to win the race. He has created a **semantic field** of exciting words to get across this idea. Find and list all these words.

To engage your audience in a presentation, you need to vary your pace (speed), volume, tone and emphasis. Find out what these words mean.

3 If you were Usain Bolt, how would you deliver this anecdote to engage your audience? Think about which words you would emphasise.

Key terms

delivery: the way a speech is presented

anecdote: a short account of an interesting or humorous incident

semantic field: a set of words that are grouped around the same topic or meaning

Developing the skills

The beginning and end of a presentation are particularly important:

- The beginning needs to gain people's interest.
- The end should be something they remember.

4 How does Usain Bolt make the beginning and the end of his anecdote effective?

Applying the skills

5 Think of an interesting memory from your life to turn into an anecdote for an audience. Think about the following:

a) What is the big idea in your anecdote and then create a semantic field based on it. For example, if the story is a sad one, include lots of words that link to sadness.

b) Look at the techniques Usain Bolt used for the beginning and end of his anecdote and try to do the same.

6 Work in pairs. Take it in turns to present and give feedback on your anecdotes. Focus on:

a) interesting content

b) effective delivery.

Checklist for success:

✔ Choose your words carefully, linking your semantic field closely to your topic.

✔ Vary the pace, volume, tone, expression and emphasis by highlighting key words/points.

✔ Practise the delivery of your opening and closing sentences.

Check your progress:

I can write a short anecdote about myself.

I can use language effectively to make my presentation interesting.

I can vary the delivery of my speech to keep my audience engaged.

Using verb tenses for effect in writing

You will learn how to:
- identify the past tense in writing
- understand different forms of past tense and apply them in your personal writing.

Personal writing is *reflective* – it often looks back at something in the past – so it is written in the past tense.

Introducing the skills

Verbs help to show if something is set in the past or present. They change tense to show in what time an action is set.

1 Copy and complete the grid of present and past verbs:

Present	Past
I *shout*	I *shouted*
He *walks*	
	They *laughed*
She *studies*	
	My father *slept*
The dolphin *swam*	

Key terms

verb: a word that expresses an action or a state of being ('look', 'go', 'feel', 'think')

Read this extract from a biography about a fighter pilot whose plane crashed in the sea.

> On the third day without water, a smudge appeared on the horizon. It grew, darkened, billowed over the rafts, and lidded the sun. Down came the rain. The men threw back their heads, spilled their bodies back, spread their arms, and opened their mouths.
>
> From *Unbroken* by Laura Hillenbrand

2 Find and list all the past tense verbs in this extract.

Developing the skills

There are different forms of the past tense.

Past tense form	Time	Example
past perfect	happened before the setting point in the past	I had eaten
past	the point of the setting	I ate
past continuous	happening in the past but not yet finished	I was eating

The past perfect and the past continuous are made up of verb phrases. These use an auxiliary verb attached to the main verb to change the tense. The two main auxiliary verbs in the past tense are 'be' and 'have':

Be	Have
I was	I had
He/she was	He/she had
We/they were	We/they had

3 Identify the verbs or verb phrases in the sentences below. Are they in the past perfect, past or past continuous tense?

a) I was sleeping comfortably.

b) He had already driven home.

c) They laughed at the film.

d) My mother was considering what to do.

e) The bird swallowed the worm in one gulp.

f) She turned the corner and bumped into her teacher.

4 Find the verbs and verb phrases in this text. Are they in the past perfect, past or past continuous tense?

> As I walked home from school, I thought about what had happened in Maths that day. The teacher was writing on the board when a bird flew in the window and bounced right off her head! I wasn't really paying attention at the time but this startled me; I had never seen anything like that before. I felt quite sorry for the teacher but it was funny.

Applying the skills

5 Think of something that happened to you this morning. Write a short account of the event. Use at least two examples of each of the past tense forms.

Check your progress:

I can convert a verb to its past tense and identify its use in writing.

I can distinguish between different forms of the past tense.

I can write about the past using different forms of the past tense.

Using vocabulary precisely in personal writing

You will learn how to:
- choose words carefully for specific meaning
- use synonyms to vary your writing.

Adjectives and adverbs add detail to writing to help the reader imagine the setting or situation more clearly.

Introducing the skills

1 Group the following words into adjectives and adverbs:

happily	warm	sweet	sweetly
precious	lazily	honest	impressively
generously	rich		

2 Find the adjectives in the following sentence:

> We have fields of wild flowers, orchards of delicious fruit, emerald mines and rivers full of trout.
>
> From *I am Malala* by Malala Yousafazai

3 Rewrite the sentence taking out all the adjectives. How do the adjectives affect the overall meaning?

4 Adverbs can change the meaning of a sentence. What is the difference in meaning between these two sentences?

a) I slept peacefully.

b) I slept terribly.

Developing the skills

Synonyms are a good way of adding variety to your writing. Remember that if words have more than one meaning, then so will their synonyms. For example, 'He is a nice man' probably means 'He is a friendly man' and 'It is a nice day' probably means 'The weather is good today'. The sentences do not mean that the man is good or that the weather is friendly.

Key terms

adjective: describes a noun (a thing)

adverb: describes a verb (usually an action)

synonym: a word that is identical or close in meaning to another word (e.g. wet/damp)

Top tip

To decide if a word is an adjective or an adverb, try using it to describe a noun or a verb. For example:

The sky is *blue*
I laughed *blue*
The sky is *loudly*
I laughed *loudly*

'Blue' only makes sense when it is used with a *noun* so it must be an *adjective*.
'Loudly' only makes sense when it is used with a *verb* so it must be an *adverb*.

The word 'nice' is often over-used in writing. Look at these synonyms for 'nice':

pleasant	enjoyable	charming	satisfying
acceptable	marvellous	delightful	lovely
agreeable	friendly	good	fine

5 Choose an accurate synonym to replace each example of the word 'nice' in this sentence:

> The view from my window is very *nice*. I can see a *nice* field with *nice* trees in it and lambs which play *nicely*.

6 Look up the following words in a thesaurus to find your own synonyms:

| happy | house | food | exercise | sad | work |
| ambition | red | walk | nature | nice | |

Applying the skills

7 Using adjectives, adverbs and synonyms, rewrite this paragraph to make the house sound *either* positive and pleasant *or* negative and scary:

> I looked at the house on the corner of the street. I walked up to the house. I opened the door and walked inside. There was a clear atmosphere inside the house. I walked down the corridor and looked into the kitchen.

Check your progress:

I can add detail in writing using adjectives and adverbs.

I can use adjectives and adverbs to change the specific meaning of writing.

I can choose synonyms to vary detail and meaning.

Linking and structuring ideas

You will learn how to:
- identify and use simple sentences
- make compound sentences using connectives.

Linking words and phrases together clearly will allow a reader to follow ideas through your writing.

> **1** Copy each of the words in the word bank and write down its meaning. For example, 'noun: a person, place or thing'.
>
> | noun | proper noun | verb | adjective | adverb | pronoun |
> |------|-------------|------|-----------|--------|---------|

Introducing the skills

There are different types of sentences. A *simple sentence* has a subject and a verb. The **subject** is the *thing* the sentence is about. It links to the verb:

The boy cried.

> **2** Copy these sentences and highlight the subject and the verb.
>
> a) The teacher laughed. b) I liked Maths.
>
> c) It flies high above us. d) We went home.
>
> e) The girl was athletic. f) She won every race.

Key terms

subject: the person or thing in a sentence that 'does' the action

Top tip

Remember – the subject is a thing (a noun), so it might be presented as a pronoun. The verb can be in any tense.

Developing the skills

Connectives are words that link parts of a sentence together:

Connective	Purpose
and	to add ideas together
but	to show contrast between ideas
or	to give an alternative
so	to lead from one idea to the next
because	to give a reason

3 Join these simple sentences together with a connective to make a **compound sentence**:

   a) I like school. I learn a lot.

   b) I must tidy up. I can't watch TV.

   c) It was very windy at lunchtime. I didn't go outside.

   d) My phone takes calls. It takes photos too.

   e) Our friends love sweets. They shouldn't eat too many.

4 Rewrite the paragraph below, choosing appropriate connectives to make it flow better. You may want to use some connectives more than once.

> This morning I woke up late. I quickly had a shower. I ate some breakfast. I grabbed my school bag. I ran out the door. I thought I was going to miss my bus! The bus was a bit slow this morning. I made it to the bus stop on time. However, I had forgotten my money. I would have to walk to school. I was going to get in trouble.

Applying the skills

5 Write a short anecdote about a specific moment in your past – for example, your first day of school.

Try to start your paragraph with a topic sentence that shows the reader the main subject of your story. In the paragraph in Question 4, 'This morning I woke up late' is the topic sentence.

Checklist for success:

✔ Use a topic sentence to give a clear idea of what each paragraph will be about.

✔ Use a mixture of simple and compound sentences so that your writing flows smoothly.

✔ Use a variety of connectives.

Key terms

compound sentence: a sentence made up of two simple sentences joined by a connective (e.g. 'I went to the beach *and* I had an ice cream.')

Check your progress:

I can identify the subject and verb in a simple sentence.

I can use connectives to make compound sentences.

I can use a variety of sentences to make my paragraphs flow.

Reflecting on writing about personal experiences

You will learn how to:
- combine the personal writing skills you have learned in one text
- understand what makes a high-level piece of personal writing.

Your task

Write a journal entry describing an event that has happened recently.

Approaching the task

A good starter sentence will help the reader understand the main idea of a piece of writing. Starter sentences will be slightly different depending on the type of personal writing.

1 Match the sentences below with a type of personal writing from the word bank.

| diary | journal | biography | autobiography |

a) William Shakespeare is recognised all over the world as a great writer.

b) I have been feeling lonely this week.

c) Today we went up into the mountains.

d) I was six years old when I first had the idea that I wanted to be famous.

2 How did you decide which type of writing went with which sentence?

3 Now draft your journal entry. Be sure to:

a) use a starter sentence that gives the reader a clue about the main idea

b) include both *explicit* and *implicit* information linked to your feelings about this event

c) choose your vocabulary carefully, using *adjectives* and *adverbs* for specific detail. Use *synonyms* for variety, to create a *semantic field* linked to your main idea

d) use different forms of the *past tense*

e) use a mixture of *simple* and *compound* sentences with *connectives*.

Response 1

> Today I had an argument with my brother. I was trying to do my homework but he kept playing his music really loud so I couldn't concentrate. I had already asked him once to turn it down but he didn't really pay any attention. When I asked him again, he just laughed and slammed the door shut!

The starter sentence makes the big idea clear.

Uses different forms of the past tense.

Uses connective to link simple sentences together.

Comment on Response 1

The paragraph links well to the starter sentence. However, this response reads more like a diary than a journal, because it only focuses on the *explicit detail* of what happened. It needs to include *implicit detail* about the writer's feelings – perhaps by using some well-chosen adjectives or adverbs.

4 Using the comments above and progress points 4b–7b in the Check your progress section at the end of this chapter, rewrite this response to improve it.

Response 2

> I could just scream at the top of my lungs! My horrible brother thinks it's so funny that I'm endlessly toiling away at silly homework but he doesn't know how unbelievably hard it is. I have tried to be reasonable but after he rudely slammed his door today, I want revenge!

Implicit clues that the writer feels angry.

Adjectives and adverbs create a semantic field linked to feelings of anger or frustration.

Interesting word choice.

Comment on Response 2

Descriptive vocabulary is used well to reveal the writer's feelings as well as implied meanings. A variety of sentence lengths keeps the reader engaged, but perhaps the use of more forms of the past tense would have made it more interesting.

5 Using the comments above and progress points 4c–7c in the Check your progress section at the end of this chapter, rewrite this response to improve it.

1a I can identify some types of personal writing.

2a I can skim a story to try and work out the writer's big idea.

3a I can scan a piece of writing to identify similes and metaphors.

4a I can write a simple anecdote about myself.

5a I can convert a verb to the past tense and identify its use in writing.

6a I can use adjectives and adverbs to add detail to my writing.

7a I can write using simple sentences.

1b I can identify the purposes of different types of personal writing.

2b I can look for clues to a writer's big idea in a starter sentence.

3b I can identify some implicit and explicit meanings in a piece of writing.

4b I can give an interesting speech, making effective use of language.

5b I can identify and use some forms of the past tense.

6b I can include implicit clues in my writing by adding adjectives and adverbs.

7b I can vary my writing by using connectives to create compound sentences.

1c I can choose suitable ideas for a piece of personal writing.

2c I can scan a story to identify the small points that reveal the writer's big idea.

3c I can create a personal response to explain what a writer is trying to tell a reader.

4c I can vary the pace, tone, expression and emphasis of a presentation to engage an audience.

5c I can accurately use different forms of the past tense in my writing.

6c I can use synonyms effectively to add meaning to my writing.

7c I can vary my words, tenses and types of sentences to engage the reader.

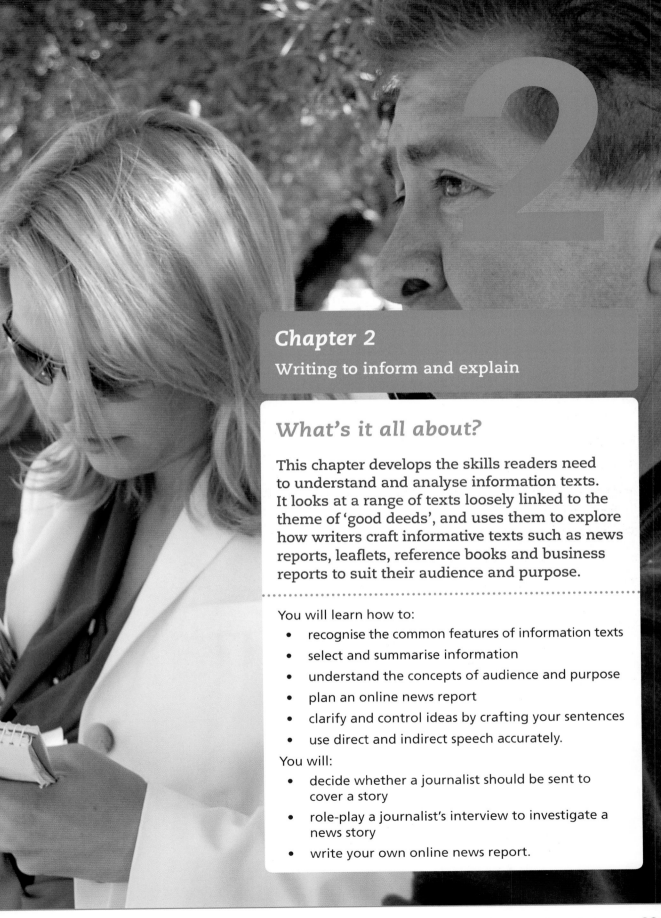

Chapter 2

Writing to inform and explain

What's it all about?

This chapter develops the skills readers need to understand and analyse information texts. It looks at a range of texts loosely linked to the theme of 'good deeds', and uses them to explore how writers craft informative texts such as news reports, leaflets, reference books and business reports to suit their audience and purpose.

You will learn how to:
- recognise the common features of information texts
- select and summarise information
- understand the concepts of audience and purpose
- plan an online news report
- clarify and control ideas by crafting your sentences
- use direct and indirect speech accurately.

You will:
- decide whether a journalist should be sent to cover a story
- role-play a journalist's interview to investigate a news story
- write your own online news report.

What is informative writing?

There are many different types of informative writing, but they usually have some common features.

Introducing the skills

Look at the two information texts on these pages. What type of text are they?

Layout features such as *headings*, *paragraphs*, *bullet points* and *images* help readers find different kinds of information quickly. Writers use the heading and first paragraph to tell readers the main topic of a text.

> **1** Read the heading and first paragraph of the following article. What is the text about?

1 **Heading** sums up what the text is about.

2 **Image** shows readers key information.

3 **First paragraph** introduces the main idea.

4 **Bullet points** express information briefly.

---

1 **Run a charity cake sale at school**

Why not raise money for your favourite **3** charity with a cake sale? Just follow these simple rules:

- Ask for permission from your head teacher.
- Agree a date, time and place for the sale.
- Advertise to students and staff.
- Ask other students to bake and bring in cakes. **4**

Developing the skills

Now read another article.

> **2** Write down the labels for the unnamed features in the second article (1, 2 and 5).

Good deed giraffe man says he likes to make others feel happy **1**

2

The Good Giraffe busks to raise money. **3**

A kind-hearted man who dresses up in a giraffe costume to

carry out random acts of kindness has said he does it because he likes to make others feel happy. **4**

Glasgow-born Armstrong Baillie, 32, also known as The Good Giraffe, has been spotted spontaneously helping random strangers across Scotland.

He was seen handing out free bananas and water to runners in the Edinburgh Half Marathon, cleaning up litter on Portobello

Beach in Edinburgh, handing out £10 vouchers to hospital patients and free coffee to cold passers-by. **5**

Mr Baillie told BBC Scotland: 'When people see me in the suit it makes them happy.' **6**

Mr Baillie, who busks to raise the funds needed to carry out his random acts of kindness, says he plans to continue making people happy. **7**

Adapted from www.metro.co.uk

The first article contains instructions for holding a charity cake sale. The second article is an online news report. They are both informative texts, with some common features and some differences.

3 What features do they share? Why do you think this is?

4 What features are found in the second article but not in the first? Why do you think this is?

3 **Caption** explains the picture.

4 **Standfirst** offers a factual summary of the news story.

5 **Middle paragraphs** give more information.

6 **Direct speech** tells readers what the people involved say.

7 **Last paragraph** brings things to a conclusion.

Applying the skills

5 Name three features that information texts share.

6 Write down all the features of an online news report.

Checklist for success:

✔ Include features of both *presentation* and *organisation* in information texts.

✔ Note common features of an online news report, as well as unique features.

Check your progress:

I can recognise the common features of information texts.

I can recognise different features in information texts.

I can recognise the conventions of an online report.

Selecting and summarising information

You will learn how to:
- use the features of a text to find information quickly
- sum up information.

You can use what you know about the common features of article writing to find and sum up information in other informative texts.

Introducing the skills

1 Read the text below, then label features 1 to 7.

Starbucks 'pay it forward' chain nearly reaches 400 acts of kindness, then one person ruins it for everyone

Woman who broke the chain said she just wanted to pay for her own drink, not anyone else's **3**

A local Starbucks in Florida saw nearly 400 people undertake an act of kindness for a complete stranger, by paying for the coffee of the person behind them in the queue. **4**

And it was all going so well; 378 people managed to 'pay it forward' at the Starbucks in St Petersburg, Florida, after one woman decided not just to pay for her own iced coffee but for the caramel macchiato ordered by the stranger behind her, too.

The person behind them then paid for the coffee of the stranger behind them, causing the chain of coffee-kindness to carry on in this manner for hours. **5**

Until one person broke it. Customer 379 on Wednesday said she just wanted to pay for her own drink – a regular coffee – and not anybody else's.

6 'I don't think she understood the concept of "pay it forward",' Celeste Guzman told ABC News. **7**

Adapted from www.independent.co.uk

Understanding the way an informative text is laid out can help you find the information in it.

2 Sum up the information given by each of the following features in the article above:

a) heading   c) standfirst

b) image   d) first paragraph.

For each feature:

- sum up briefly the information it provides. For example: 'Image shows Starbucks coffee cups'

- decide what this information adds to the text. For example: 'Image shows that cups of coffee are important in this news story'.

Developing the skills

To find information in a text, scan it to identify features that give certain types of details. For example:

- speech marks will help you find people's views
- words beginning with a capital letter will identify people, places, days or brands
- numbers will tell you dates, costs, ages or times.

3 Copy and complete the grid below to answer the questions about the Starbucks article.

Question	Answer	What helped you find the answer?
a) On which day of the week did the 'chain' break?		
b) How many people successfully completed the chain?		
c) Why did the Starbucks' spokesperson believe the 'chain' broke?		
d) What was the name of the Starbucks' spokesperson?		

Applying the skills

4 Sum up in as few words as you can how the 'pay it forward' chain works.

Check your progress:

I can use clues to find information.

I can use the features of information texts to find details.

I can scan a text to find information efficiently and sum it up.

Understanding the audience and purpose of informative texts

You will learn how to:
- recognise ways that texts are crafted to suit their purpose and audience
- suggest reasons for writers' choices.

Informative writers craft their texts carefully to suit both their **audience** (for example, customers or officials) and their **purpose** (for example, to entertain or update the reader).

Key terms

audience: the group of people that a text is written for

purpose: what the writer wants the text to achieve

Introducing the skills

1 Look through Texts A, B and C in this section. Which statement below do you think best describes the audience and purpose of each text?

a) to interest adults

b) to inform team leaders

c) to report to officials.

Read Text A. Notice how the heading tells officials that this section contains information on what the charity has done. 'Achievements' suggests the charity has been successful. 'Our' makes the audience feel they have played a part in this success.

Text A

Our Achievements

Thanks in large part to our campaigning, free school meals will be available to all infant school children, helping hundreds of thousands of families in poverty. Important **amendments** to the Children and Families **Bill** and Care Bill mean that young carers will now be protected from taking on family caring duties that could **adversely affect** their education and childhood.

From The Children's Society annual report

Vocabulary

amendments: changes

bill: law

adversely affect: harm

Now read Texts B and C.

Text B

'How I resolved to be a better person': Mum's 365 good deeds in a year.

Mum-of-three Judith O'Reilly has done everything from clearing up a dead mouse to helping the homeless.

In 12 months, and 365 good deeds, Judith, 48 has done everything from clearing up a dead mouse to helping the homeless and trying to join a lifeboat crew, even though she is a poor swimmer – all with varying degrees of success.

Judith admits: 'I'm a terrible swimmer. If someone had needed hauling out of the water in a stormy sea, all I think I'd have been capable of doing is asking if they had any last words.'

Her deeds ranged from the **mundane** to the mad. She got rid of a dead mouse from the trap in a neighbour's kitchen, volunteered in a hospital shop and joined nuns making soup for the homeless.

Judith even helped a blind old lady off a train – only realising later that she had failed to check which station the woman actually wanted to get off at.

Adapted from www.mirror.co.uk

Text C

What is a 'good turn' and what should you teach your troops?

First of all... a good turn is simply a good deed. It's something a Girl Scout does without expecting recognition or praise. Of course, as a troop leader, make a point to praise the girls for doing good turns. They need that **positive reinforcement**... no matter what age... no matter if they just shrug it off and say 'no biggie'.

Adapted from http://girlscoutleader101.blogspot.co.uk

2 Complete these sentences to explain how the headings in Text B and Text C suit their different audiences and purposes.

   a) Text B's heading tells…[who?] the article is about…[what?]. The word…suggests…

   b) Text C's heading tells…[who?] the blog is about…[what?]. The word…suggests…

3 Text A does not include an image, but Text B does. Why do you think this is?

4 How does the image help Text B achieve its purpose?

Developing the skills

Formal English is usually used in official texts. Informal English is used for texts without an official purpose. This grid shows language features of formal and informal English.

Language feature	Formal English	Informal English
abbreviations (missing letters in words are marked by an apostrophe – I'm = I am)	no	yes
expressive punctuation **single dash** – to introduce a comment **ellipsis** … to suggest a longer pause or unexpressed thoughts **exclamation mark !** to show surprise or pleasure **brackets ( )** to include a comment from the writer **CAPITAL LETTERS** to give emphasis to whole words	no	yes
slang and idioms	only expressions that every reader will understand	yes
official terms and names	yes	sometimes

Vocabulary

mundane: ordinary

positive reinforcement: a reward for doing the behaviour that is wanted

5 Read Texts A, B and C again and find examples of the features listed. Record your findings in a grid like the one below.

Feature	Text A	Text B	Text C
abbreviations	none	I'm, I'd	
expressive punctuation			

Writers choose to use formal or informal English depending on the purpose and audience of their text. For example, the writer of Text C uses informal English to sound friendly and knowledgeable, so readers would listen to their advice.

6 The writer of Text A uses formal English. How does this suit the purpose of the text?

Applying the skills

Re-read Text B.

7 Explain how the use of direct speech suits the audience of this news report.

8 Has the writer used formal or informal English when writing Judith's speech? Why do you think the writer made this choice?

9 Why might the writer have used mostly formal English to write the article?

Checklist for success:

✔ Decide how each language feature affects the audience.

✔ Distinguish between formal and informal English by checking for slang, abbreviations and the use of punctuation.

Check your progress:

I can recognise the ways in which a text suits its readers or purpose.

I can recognise formal and informal English in a text.

I can suggest reasons why writers' choices suit their audience and purpose.

Responding to informative texts

You will learn how to:

- combine the reading skills you have learned when responding to an informative text
- understand what makes a high-level response to informative writing.

Your task

The editor of an online newspaper called *Top Stories* is looking for a journalist to write some engaging online news reports that will touch readers' hearts. The newspaper is read by English-speaking adults all over the world.

Read the article below to decide how well this journalist's writing would suit *Top Stories*.

Target Employee's Good Deed Goes Viral

If you can't tie a tie, maybe you should find a Target guy.

That's what one young job seeker who walked into a Raleigh, North Carolina Target store did this week.

The teen, who was searching for a clip-on tie before his first job interview, was disappointed to find out the store didn't have any.

But instead of sending him on his way, Target employee Dennis Roberts picked out a tie from a rack, brought it to the teen and taught him how to tie it.

A shopper who witnessed the simple act of kindness found the sight so heart-warming, she had to share it.

Audrey Mark posted a photo she took of the pair inside the store, along with the background story, on Target's Facebook page to thank the 'awesome' employee who helped the teen out.

The Facebook post was shared by more than 4,000 people, received 50,000 likes and nearly 1,200 comments.

Aside from helping the boy with a tie and telling him to tuck in his shirt, Roberts and fellow Target employee Cathy Scott offered some job interview advice.

Target said Roberts and Scott are just two of the countless employees who make 'Target uniquely Target'.

"Our team members love going above and beyond every day for our guests," Target Public Relations spokeswoman Kristen Emmons told CBS News.

As if the story couldn't be any more heartwarming, the jobseeker received dozens of cheers and good luck wishes as he exited the store.

Hundreds of touched Facebook users also wished the boy luck on his interview, which apparently took place at a Chick-fil-A nearby.

"Fingers crossed for this [kid's] interview!" Mark wrote. "Hope he got the job," one user wrote. "I certainly hope you got the job you sought, but you deserve so much more," another wrote.

Whether the teen lands the job or not, at least he'll be better prepared for the future. "We're rooting for him in his interviews," Emmons said. "And by the way, we love his tie."

From www.cbsnews.com

Approaching the task

Complete these tasks to find evidence in the text that will help you decide whether the journalist is suitable for the job at *Top Stories*.

1 Read and sum up the story in your own words.

   a) Who posted the story online?

   b) Where did the event happen?

   c) How many people liked the story?

   d) Will *Top Stories* readers find this engaging and touching?

2 Think about the conventions of an online news report.

   a) Which conventions has the journalist included?

   b) Name any conventions that are missing.

   c) How well does the image suit the text's audience and purpose?

3 Think about the style of writing.

    a) Find two pieces of evidence that show whether the writer has written in formal or informal English.

    b) How well will this article suit 'English-speaking adults all over the world'?

4 Now use your answers to help you write a paragraph explaining whether or not you think the editor of *Top Stories* should employ this journalist. You could start like this:

> The editor should/should not employ this
> journalist because…

Reflecting on your progress

Response 1

> The editor should employ this journalist because
> **1** the story is about a teenager who could not buy a clip
> on tie and this will touch readers who feel sorry for him. **2**
> The writer has done a good job and included all the
> **3** conventions of an online news report. The image is helpful
> because it shows what a clip-on tie looks like, which
> readers might not know. The writer has used formal **4**
> English so all English-speaking readers everywhere will
> understand the report.

1 Does not sum up accurately wha the story is about

2 Tries to explains how text's content suits audience.

3 Does not notice that some conventions are missing.

4 Recognises that only formal English is used and why this suit readers.

Comment on Response 1

The paragraph includes all the information that the task asked for. The student also uses details from the text to show some understanding of how writers use conventions and craft texts to suit audience and purpose. However, this student has not summed up the story accurately – only focusing on one part of it. The whole story includes the fact that the Target employee's good deed was rapidly seen by a lot of people on Facebook.

5 Using the comments above and progress points 1b–3b in the Check your progress section at the end of this chapter, rewrite this response to improve it.

Response 2

The editor should not employ this journalist because **1** although the good deed is a touching story, **the fact the story was popular is not very interesting but the title makes that the most important thing.** Additionally, the image does not explain the story. **Readers do not need to know what a clip-on tie looks like.** **2** It would be best to show the customer or the employees involved, but even the Facebook page would be more suitable. **3** The first paragraph does not sum up the story, and there is no speech giving people's views about the event. There is just a Target spokesperson boasting about how wonderful their company is.

1 Clearly understands what the story is about and sums it up.

2 Explains why the image does not suit the purpose and shows understanding by suggesting what would be better.

3 Recognises which conventions are missing and that the speech that is present is not adding to the story, but just providing an ending to the article.

Comment on Response 2

This response shows that the student understands the text and has thought carefully about how well it suits its audience and purpose. The student has also explained clearly which conventions of an online news report are being followed and used effectively, and which are not. However, the response does not include information about whether the writer's choice of language is formal or informal.

6 Using the comments above and progress points 1c–3c in the Check your progress section at the end of this chapter, rewrite this response to improve it.

Interviewing to gather news

You will learn how to:
- take part in a role play
- listen politely and talk effectively in an interview.

People who do well in **interviews** listen carefully so they can work out how to answer a question clearly and effectively.

Introducing the skills

You are going to work in pairs to act out a scene in which a journalist interviews someone who has done a good deed.

During the interview, the journalist needs to find out:

- what the good deed was
- what happened when the good deed was carried out
- details about the people involved – their full names, ages, and so on
- where events happened
- how the people involved feel about their part in the event.

Key terms

interview: a conversation in which an interviewer asks someone questions

1 In your pairs, decide which role each of you will play, then plan your ideas.

a) **Interviewer:** make a list of questions to ask that cover everything in the brief (e.g. 'What is your full name?').

b) **Interviewee:** work out in detail what you will say about each of the bullet points above.

You will need to listen carefully to each other without interrupting. What you say should link to what has just been said – you should answer the question or ask for more detail. You also need to be polite to each other. For example:

Please could you tell me…

That's an interesting question…

Thank you for agreeing to answer my questions.

Thank you for inviting me…

2 Practise the interview, following your plan and using the polite phrases above.

Developing the skills

Now develop your interview.

3 What other questions or information could you include to improve your interview?

4 As the interviewer, show how well you have listened by linking what you say to what you have heard.

   a) Re-state what you heard as a question to check you have understood ('So what happened was…?').

   b) Comment on what you heard ('That sounds exciting…').

   c) Ask for more detail ('What was…like?').

During your interview:

- smile and look each other in the eye when you shake hands in greeting

- look at each other as you talk and listen

- your facial expression should show you are responding to what is being said – smile and nod when you agree, look concerned if you hear something sad.

5 How could these students improve their gestures?

Applying the skills

6 Carry out your interview for a final time, using all the skills you have learned.

Checklist for success:

✔ Listen carefully and make sure what you say links to what you have heard.

✔ Show politeness and interest through your language, eyes and expression.

Check your progress:

I can take part in a role-play interview.

I can use words to show I am listening carefully to what someone is saying.

I can use words and gestures to show I am listening carefully.

Planning an online news report

You will learn how to:
- plan an online news report to suit a wide audience
- develop a paragraph plan for your text.

Planning the content and organisation of your text is vital so that it will achieve its purpose and suit its audience.

Introducing the skills

You are going to write an engaging online news report about someone's unusual good deed, for a worldwide English-speaking audience.

1 First, think of some possible ideas for your story by writing a list of general 'good deeds'. For example:

> Helping someone find something they lost.
> Doing something to raise money for charity.
> Helping to solve someone's problem.

Using your list as a starting point, make a note of five more specific good deeds – for example, finding a lost key.

Next you need to work out what could make a good deed unusual. Think about:

- why the good deed was needed (e.g. a wedding dress was destroyed in a fire two weeks before the wedding)
- the person who did the good deed (e.g. a schoolgirl)
- the activity (e.g. found a replacement wedding dress)
- their reason for helping (e.g. read about the bride's loss and felt sorry for her)
- how the deed was done (e.g. the schoolgirl got all her friends to ask their grandmothers if they had kept their wedding dress).

2 Choose two of your specific good deeds and use the bullet points above to help you decide what makes them unusual.

3 Decide on your best idea, then work out the details of the story using a grid like the one below. Answer the questions as fully as you can.

Question	Details to include in article
What was the good deed?	Ariana replaced bride's (Precious's) vintage 1950s lace wedding dress, which had been destroyed in a fire at her home two weeks before the wedding.
How was it done?	Ariana and her friends contacted their oldest relatives to see if any had kept their wedding dresses. Ariana's Great Aunt Rose had.
Why did the person do the good deed?	
What happened as a result?	

Your online news report should identify people in the story by stating their full name, age and where they come from (their home town and country), because you are writing for an international audience.

4 Note the details you will use to identify each person in your report.

Reports include people's reaction to events. For example, Ariana's Great Aunt Rose might be reported as saying: 'It was lovely to see my old wedding dress make a new bride so happy. I'm glad I kept it!'

5 Decide how each person you are reporting on would answer the question: 'How do you feel about your part in the story?'

Developing the skills

Online news reports contain three types of paragraphs:

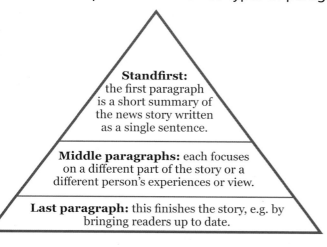

Standfirst: the first paragraph is a short summary of the news story written as a single sentence.

Middle paragraphs: each focuses on a different part of the story or a different person's experiences or view.

Last paragraph: this finishes the story, e.g. by bringing readers up to date.

6 List the information that you will mention in the middle paragraphs of your news story. Make sure that events are both explained and commented on by the people involved. For example:

Paragraph topics

Why Ariana got involved.

How the girls searched by asking their oldest relatives.

How Precious felt when she saw the wedding dress.

Great Aunt Rose's view about giving Precious her dress to wear.

7 Decide the order in which you will write your paragraph topics and number them in that order.

Now you need to make a paragraph plan by deciding what details to include in each paragraph. For example:

Topic of paragraph	Details to include
Why Ariana got involved	Ariana read about Precious losing her wedding dress in a newspaper report about the fire.
	Ariana remembered seeing her grandmothers' black and white photograph of her wedding day.
	Ariana felt very sorry for Precious.

8 Make a detailed paragraph plan for each middle paragraph for your online news report.

Connectives are used to show readers how a paragraph links to the one before. In the example below, the connective 'However' shows that there is a *contrast* between the information in this paragraph and the one before:

> ...after the fire any hope of a happy wedding seemed impossible.
>
> However, Ariana Oladatun, 15 of Cookstown, Nigeria, read about Precious's misery...

Key terms

connective: a word or phrase used to link parts of a sentence or to show a connection between two paragraphs

The grid below contains some examples of connectives.

Connective	Links paragraphs by
At first / Soon / After that / Now	showing time has passed
Nearby / Not far away	showing distance between events
Additionally / In the same way	adding an idea to a previous one
However / But	contrasting an idea with the last paragraph

9 Decide which connectives you will use to begin three of your middle paragraphs.

10 The last paragraph should bring the reader up to date, so decide on the latest news for your event (e.g. 'Now Ariana hopes to give the vintage dress a third outing – on her own wedding day.') and plan what to tell your readers in your last paragraph.

Applying the skills

11 Check your plan for your online news report thoroughly. Add in any missing details, and choose a suitable connective to begin your last paragraph.

Check your progress:

I can plan a news story that will interest readers.

I can plan the sequence of paragraphs to tell the news story in an interesting way.

I can plan paragraphs and choose connectives to show how they link.

Checklist for success:

✔ Choose an interesting news story for your readers.

✔ Plan the content of the standfirst, the middle paragraphs and conclusion.

✔ Choose appropriate connectives to link each paragraph.

Clarifying and controlling ideas through language

You will learn how to:
- write a variety of sentences accurately
- craft sentences for effect.

Writers of news reports choose a variety of sentence types to express different types of information and keep their readers engaged.

Introducing the skills

The standfirst sums up the story, telling readers who did what, when and where. This can be a simple sentence (also called a main **clause**) with a subject verb and object in this order:

> Ariana Oladatun found a wedding dress.

1 Write your news story as a short simple sentence like the example above.

A standfirst includes precise information about the people, event, place and time. This grid shows a pattern that the standfirst could follow.

Key terms

clause: a group of words that include a verb

Subject – the person doing the action or event.

Verb – expressing the action or event.

Object – the person or thing receiving the action of the verb.

Order of information	Example	Type of words
1 Subject (full name of the person the sentence is about)	Ariana Oladatun,	proper noun
2 Age	age 15,	adjective
3 Place (where from)	from Cookstown,	preposition + proper noun
4 Verb (expressing what the subject did)	found	verb in past tense
5 Object (who and/or what received the subject's action)	a replacement wedding dress for Precious Bonita, 21,	noun phrase (adjective + noun)
6 Time (when)	after a blaze destroyed her original one two weeks before her wedding day.	preposition (time) + noun phrase

2 Write your standfirst following the pattern of information in the grid.

Developing the skills

A text written only in simple sentences sounds stilted. Vary your sentences by using **conjunctions** to join clauses. The grid below gives you some examples.

Key terms

conjunction: a word that joins clauses in a sentence

First clause	Conjunction	Second clause	Effect of chosen conjunction
Ariana told her friends to ask their older relatives	and	the whole class joined in the search.	'and' emphasises how many people got involved.
Ariana told her friends to ask their older relatives	but	the whole class joined in the search.	'but' emphasises that what happened was unexpected.
The class asked relatives if they still had their wedding dress	or	whether relatives had the pattern used to sew it.	'or' introduces alternatives, making readers wonder what happened next.
Ariana was amazed	because	her Great Aunt Rose still had hers.	'because' shows readers they will discover the reason for Arianna's amazement.

3 Write four sentences of your own using each of the four conjunctions to create different effects.

Main clause (makes sense on its own).

Subordinate clause (does not make sense on its own).

Applying the skills

4 Now write your report, using the skills you have learned in this topic.

Check your progress:

I can write a detailed simple sentence.

I can use connectives to construct different types of sentences.

I can craft my sentences by choosing connectives to create an effect on my reader.

Checklist for success:

✔ Pack your standfirst sentence with details.

✔ Vary your sentences by using connectives.

✔ Choose connectives carefully to create different effects.

Using direct and indirect speech to inform

You will learn how to:
- punctuate direct speech in a sentence
- include indirect speech in a sentence.

Online news reports may quote people's views using the words they actually spoke (*direct* speech) or sum up what was said as *indirect* or *reported* speech.

Introducing the skills

In a news report, journalists only include the most important words someone says. They set them out like this:

> Precious Bonita said, 'The blaze was a nightmare. I am so grateful to Ariana for making my dream wedding possible.'

Start by saying who is speaking. Then place a comma before the speech begins.

Open the speech marks before writing the words spoken. Remember to close the speech marks at the end of the speech.

In direct speech, the speaker uses personal pronouns such as 'I', 'my', 'mine' and the first person form of verbs.

Write the spoken words as a sentence beginning with a capital letter and ending with a full stop, question mark or exclamation mark.

1 Read the instructions next to the example carefully, then answer these questions:

a) Where do the speech marks go?

b) If you begin the sentence by saying who is speaking, what punctuation should you use before the opening speech mark?

c) What punctuation should the first spoken word begin with?

d) What punctuation is needed before closing the speech mark?

2 Rewrite the direct speech below, adding the five missing punctuation marks:

> Rose Oladatun, aged 80, said i hope Precious' marriage is as happy as mine was

3 Write two sentences for your online news report that include direct speech.

Developing the skills

Sometimes a writer reports what someone says by simply summing it up. This is *indirect* or *reported* speech. No speech marks are needed – just follow the usual rules for punctuating sentences.

This example shows a pattern you can follow to write indirect speech:

> Rose Oladatun said that she was delighted to lend Precious her dress and hoped the marriage would be as happy as her own had been.

Start your sentence with the name of the person whose speech you will report.

Introduce indirect speech with 'said *that*', 'stated *that*' or 'explained *that*'.

Refer to the speaker in the third person when summing up their speech.

Write verbs referring to the speaker in the third person.

4 Rewrite these sentences as indirect speech:

a) Precious said, 'Ariana's thoughtfulness is an inspiration.'

b) Rose said, 'The wedding brought back many happy memories.'

5 Write a paragraph of indirect speech for your online news report.

Applying the skills

6 Write two versions of the speaker's words below for a news report. One paragraph should include direct speech, the other should use indirect speech.

I asked everyone in my class to contact their older relatives to see if they had kept their wedding dresses.

Checklist for success:

✔ Only use speech marks for direct speech.

✔ Punctuate the beginning and end of direct speech.

✔ Use 'said that' and third-person verbs when using indirect speech.

Check your progress:

I can understand the difference between direct speech and indirect speech.

I can punctuate and express direct speech accurately in a report.

I can punctuate and express both direct and indirect speech accurately in a report.

Writing an online news report

You will learn how to:
- combine the informative writing skills you have learned in one text
- understand what makes a high-level piece of informative writing.

Your task

Write an online news report about a project called 'One Good Deed Every Day', which challenges teenagers to do a good deed each day and record it on the project's website. Your report must be engaging and written to suit young English-speaking adults from anywhere in the world.

Approaching the task

1 Plan the general content of your report. Include:

   a) who set up the project and why

   b) examples of good deeds done by students

   c) people's response to the project (e.g. those who have been helped by it, education experts)

   d) any other ideas you have.

2 Now plan your report in more detail, thinking about what you will include in your paragraphs and various layout features:

   a) heading   d) final paragraph

   b) standfirst   e) image.

   c) middle paragraphs

3 You will also need to include on your plan details such as people's full names, ages, home town, and their views (in direct/indirect speech).

4 Now write your online news report.

Reflecting on your progress

Read the examples on the next page of students' online news reports.

Response 1

Teenagers are doing One Good Deed Every Day.

Teacher Brett Mark, 50, from England set up the challenge.

Teenagers have bought hamburgers for homeless people, found owners of dropped wallets and rescued trapped animals. 'My favourite good deed was helping parents find their toddler.'

Teenagers can record their good deeds on the OGDED website. They have to prove they did the deed. Photographs can be uploaded.

The first sentence sums up the story, but does not give much detail.

Each paragraph tells a new part of the story, but not in the best order.

Direct speech used but it is not clear who spoke.

All the sentences are simple sentences.

Comment on Response 1

The response explains what the teenagers are doing quite clearly and includes a comment from one of the teenagers.

5 Using the comments above and progress points 4b–7b in the Check your progress section at the end of this chapter, rewrite this response to improve it.

Response 2

Natalia Begum, aged 31, from Cameroon, asked millions of teenagers worldwide to do One Good Deed Every Day.

Every day, teenagers post a description of their good deed on the OGDED website and add proof such as a photograph.

Begum explains, 'It's good because teenagers discover they can make a difference to their world.'

Some favourite good deeds are: babysitting, sweeping up snow or leaves from neighbours' gardens and helping older relatives with computer problems. The most unusual was helping to move a stranded dolphin back into the sea.

A detailed standfirst sums up the story.

Paragraphs are in an effective sequence.

Uses accurately punctuated direct speech in informal English.

Connectives are used to build the sentences.

Comment on Response 2

This response tells the story well in a series of paragraphs that include interesting details. To develop it further, the student needs to cover more points – for example, more than one teenager's experiences in detail.

6 Using the comments above and progress points 4c–7c in the Check your progress section at the end of this chapter, rewrite this response to improve it.

Check your progress

1a I can identify some common features of information text.

2a I can use a text's clues to find information.

3a I can explain how a text suits its readers or purpose.

4a I can take part in a role-play interview.

5a I can plan and write a news story that will interest readers.

6a I can write an effective simple sentence.

7a I can recognise the difference between direct speech and indirect speech.

1b I can recognise features of presentation and organisation in information texts.

2b I can use the organisation features of a text to find details.

3b I can identify formal and informal English in a text.

4b I can listen carefully to what someone is saying to extract information.

5b I can plan and write an engaging news story that will interest readers.

6b I can write different types of sentences using connectives accurately.

7b I can use and accurately punctuate direct speech in my writing.

1c I can identify features of information texts and the conventions of online reports.

2c I can scan a text to find relevant details and sum them up.

3c I can explain how and why a text suits its audience and purpose.

4c I can use words and gestures to show I have listened carefully.

5c I can plan and craft a sequence of paragraphs, using connectives, to write an engaging online news report.

6c I can craft my sentences to have a particular effect on my reader.

7c I can use and accurately punctuate direct and indirect speech in my writing.

Chapter 3
Writing to argue and persuade

What's it all about?

This chapter develops the skills needed to write persuasively. It looks at a range of texts on the theme of whether zoos are good or bad, and uses them to explore the techniques writers use when creating persuasive or argumentative texts such as adverts or campaigns.

You will learn how to:
- identify the purpose of a text
- use inference to explain the implicit and explicit meanings of words
- use quotations to support your ideas
- comment on a writer's word choices
- use complex sentences to develop ideas
- rearrange your sentences to create different effects
- use persuasive techniques in your writing
- structure an argument in a clear way.

You will:
- write a paragraph for a zoo's website
- take part in a group discussion about whether zoos should be banned
- write a letter to a newspaper arguing for or against keeping animals in zoos.

What is writing to argue and persuade?

You will learn how to:
- identify the purpose of persuasive and argumentative texts
- use adjectives to present a positive view.

Texts that have a clear point of view are sometimes called *persuasive* texts or *argumentative* texts. They are designed to make the reader think carefully about an issue.

Introducing the skills

Persuasive texts present one point of view. Adverts – whether they are on posters, television, leaflets or websites – are persuasive because they are trying to sell you a product or encourage you to use something.

Look at this text from the London Zoo website. The writer wants to make 'Gorilla Kingdom' sound attractive to potential visitors, so they emphasise its best aspects and use positive vocabulary to make it sound like a thrilling experience:

Our Gorilla Kingdom brings the African rainforest to the heart of London. You'll be able to meet Africa's <u>most exciting</u> residents, featuring our colony of western lowland gorillas. With <u>breathtakingly close</u> views, this is one encounter <u>you'll be sure to remember</u>.

From www.zsl.org

Texts that *argue* need to consider both sides of the argument. However, this does not mean that they are balanced. The writer has their own point of view and only considers the opposing viewpoint so that they can dismiss it and make their own argument sound more convincing. Argumentative texts might be feature articles, letters to newspapers, speeches or essays.

Read the opening to a feature article below. In it, the writer considers why people might *like* to visit zoos before dismissing this idea.

It is more than 180 years since the first zoos opened in Britain. To put that in perspective, the electric telegraph hadn't been invented, never mind the telephone, and passenger railways had only just come into existence.

People rarely travelled far, hardly ever abroad, so imagine their delight when they visited menageries filled with chimpanzees, oryx and orangutans.

I can also understand why so many of you today want to take your children to see an elephant or giraffe or gorilla close up.

But I think the time has come to re-evaluate the role of zoos. I know it's not practical to close all zoos today. Nor am I suggesting that all zoos can be closed tomorrow. But I am proposing that we phase them out over the next 20 to 30 years.

From www.dailymail.co.uk

1 Look at the first highlighted sentence. Which point of view does the writer sympathise with?

2 Look at the second highlighted sentence. Which word signals that the previous point of view is not the writer's own?

Developing the skills

Read the following three extracts, which all express a point of view.

Text A

There are p-p-plenty of penguins at ZSL London Zoo in our stunning Penguin Beach exhibit – England's biggest penguin pool!

From www.zsl.org

Text B

Of course, there have been LOTS of changes to the world's biodiversity over time. Part of the process of evolution means that some species will go extinct and new ones will evolve to fit into changing environments. But that process normally happens over very long periods of time. Typically, only a few species go extinct over the course of 100 or even 1,000 years.

From www.kidsdiscover.com

Text C

Why do zoos matter? Basically, because we care. Because we want to keep this planet's amazing wildlife around for future generations.

From www.stlzoo.org

3 For each text, say whether it is persuasive or argumentative.

4 What do you notice about the word choices in Texts A and C? How do the writers make the zoos sound like good places to visit?

5 How does the writer of Text B make their point of view sound convincing?

When writing to persuade, you need to use positive language. **Adjectives** are very useful in creating a positive image – for example, '*amazing* wildlife', '*biggest* penguin pool'.

When writing to argue, it is important to use evidence to make your point of view sound convincing. A piece of argumentative writing will usually be longer and more developed than a persuasive piece, so make sure you have lots of examples to back up your points and keep your argument going. For example:

> Typically, only *a few species go extinct over the course of 100 or even 1,000 years.*

Applying the skills

6 Write the opening paragraph for the homepage of a zoo's website. Remember – you are trying to persuade people to come and visit the zoo.

You could start like this:

> Ever wondered why a…is so playful? Well now you can find out at…

Check your progress:

Checklist for success:

✔ Highlight the best aspects of the zoo.

✔ Use adjectives to 'sell' a positive image of the zoo.

✔ Mention a range of features to make the zoo sound appealing.

I can identify some features of a persuasive text.

I can explain how positive adjectives are used in persuasive texts.

I can recognise the features of a persuasive text and identify its purpose.

Making inferences from persuasive texts

You will learn how to:
- identify the purpose of a text
- use inference to explain the implicit and explicit meanings of words.

Writers choose their words carefully. Knowing the **literal** meaning of the words and the deeper meaning behind them will help you understand a writer's viewpoint. It will also help you understand the purpose of the text.

Key terms

literal: the most basic or usual meaning of a word; its explicit meaning

1 Have you ever been to a zoo? Do you think they are a good idea? Using the picture for ideas, write down three benefits of zoos.

The text below is from the website of the Saint Louis Zoo, in the United States. It is explaining 'Why Zoos Matter'.

The world around us is changing fast. Species of wildlife are facing global extinction on a massive scale. About 21% of the world's mammal species, about 12% of the bird species and about 33% of all amphibian species are threatened with extinction. Cranes and cheetahs, great apes and rhinos and so many more are in trouble. Zoos are in a unique position to make a difference.

Zoos deal with living creatures. We work with an incredible variety of animals, from one-celled creatures to elephants. Our research on behavior, reproductive biology, nutrition, animal health and genetics is valuable to wildlife managers, field researchers and other scientists.

For example, the Saint Louis Zoo has been doing a mother/infant bonding study with antelope and other hoofed animals at Red Rocks for 14 years. The data we've gathered – how often and when a species typically nurses, who initiates nursing, proximity, grooming, nuzzling – has provided information to field researchers that would be hard to come by otherwise.

From www.stlzoo.org

2   Write down all the words from the article that tell us that the world's wildlife is in danger.

3   Find places in the text where you could use the following synonyms:

    a) in danger

    b) big

    c) sole.

4   What difference would using these words, rather than the original ones, make to the impact of the passage? How important does the zoo's work seem now?

5   Think about the writer's choice of particular words:

    a) Why is the word 'threatened' better than the phrase 'in danger'?

    b) Why is the word 'massive' better than the word 'big'?

    c) What does the word 'unique' mean?

    d) What does the word 'unique' hint about the zoo?

6   What does the writer want the reader to think about the zoo?

The writer uses powerful words to make the zoo's work seem essential and persuade the reader that zoos are good for the world's wildlife. When you analyse a text, you need to identify and write about these powerful words and the effect that they have. You can do this by explaining the *explicit meaning* of words and by using inference to work out the *implied meanings*.

Developing the skills

7   Choose one of the following phrases:

    a) 'facing global extinction'

    b) 'unique position'

    c) 'Zoos deal with living creatures'.

Write an explanation of its *explicit* meaning. Try to use only one word or a short phrase. For example:

The phrase 'facing global extinction' means that species of wildlife *could be wiped out*.

Use the starter sentence:

> The phrase '…' means that…

Now consider what the phrase you have chosen hints at about zoos. This is the *implied* meaning. For example:

> This hints that without zoos, some wildlife will be destroyed.

8 Add a sentence to your first one that explains what your chosen phrase hints at about zoos. Use the starter sentence:

> This hints that…

Now think about how the phrase links to the *purpose* of the text – the idea that zoos are essential. For example:

> Therefore, the writer implies that zoos are essential because without their help, some wildlife will not survive.

9 Add to your paragraph by writing a sentence that links your phrase to the purpose of the text. Use the following starter sentence to help you:

> Therefore, the writer implies that zoos are essential because…

10 When you have finished, swap paragraphs with a partner. They should check that you have explained the meanings clearly and without repeating yourself.

11 Write a paragraph about a powerful word or phrase from the following extract:

> Why do zoos matter? Basically, because we care. Because we want to keep this planet's amazing wildlife around for future generations.

Use these starter sentences to help you:

> The word/phrase '…' means…
> This word/phrase hints that…
> Therefore, the writer implies that zoos are…

Checklist for success:

✔ Only use one word or a short phrase to explain the explicit meaning.

✔ Explain what the word/phrase hints at (implicit meaning).

✔ Link the word/phrase to the purpose of the text.

✔ Do not repeat words from the passage in your explanations.

Check your progress:

I can identify the purpose of a persuasive text.

I can comment on both the explicit and implicit meanings of words.

I can link my comments about the explicit and implicit meanings of words to a writer's purpose.

Using quotations as evidence

You will learn how to:

- use quotations to support your ideas
- comment on a writer's word choices.

To argue convincingly, you need to back up your ideas with evidence. The best evidence to use when writing about a text is a quotation.

Introducing the skills

Read this text from London Zoo's website, describing 'Penguin Beach'.

There are p-p-plenty of penguins at ZSL London Zoo in our stunning Penguin Beach exhibit – England's biggest penguin pool!

The new exhibit features a large pool with stunning underwater viewing areas so you can see how our flippered friends fly under water. The exhibit's 1200 sq metre pool holds 450,000 litres of water!

Our large demonstration area turns feeding time in to an even bigger spectacle than before. Penguin Beach Live will feature twice daily feeds where visitors can watch the birds diving for their food.

From www.zsl.org

1 Find three words or phrases that the writer uses to make Penguin Beach sound impressive.

It is important to write down your evidence correctly. Copy the words from the text exactly and use quotation marks around those words. For example: 'an even bigger spectacle'.

2 Write out the words or phrases, following these rules.

You should also include an introductory sentence before you write the quotation. The words you use in the introductory sentence should come from the question. For example:

> The writer makes Penguin Beach sound impressive by using the words, 'even bigger spectacle'.

3 Write out one of your examples again, using an introductory sentence like the one above.

Developing the skills

4 Which of these statements best explains the implied meaning of the phrase 'even bigger spectacle'?

a) It suggests that Penguin Beach was already extraordinary but is now better still.

b) It implies that Penguin Beach is larger than it was.

A good answer will also explain the *effects* of the word choices in the quotation.

5 What does the word 'spectacle' imply about Penguin Beach? Find its meaning in a dictionary if you need to. Write your answer as a single sentence beginning:

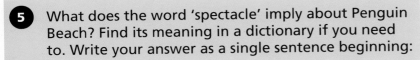

> The word 'spectacle' tells the reader that
> Penguin Beach is...

Applying the skills

Read this text about Gorilla Kingdom.

Our Gorilla Kingdom brings the African rainforest to the heart of London. You'll be able to meet Africa's most exciting residents, featuring our colony of western lowland gorillas. With breathtakingly close views, this is one encounter you'll be sure to remember.

When you step into this atmospheric exhibit, you'll first be able to explore our **African aviary** before moving on into our Gorilla Kingdom. This natural and engaging environment is home to our gorillas, featuring a stunning clearing, their own personal island, and an indoor gymnasium.

From www.zsl.org

6 Write a short paragraph showing how the writer uses language to make Gorilla Kingdom sound appealing.

Checklist for success:

- ✔ Use one accurate quotation as evidence.
- ✔ Explain what the quotation suggests.
- ✔ Explain the effect of an individual word.

Check your progress:

I can choose a suitable quotation to support an idea.

I can identify the implied meaning of a writer's choice of words.

I can select a range of quotations from a text and explain the effect of the writer's language.

Responding to persuasive texts

You will learn how to:

- combine the reading skills you have learned when responding to a persuasive text
- understand what makes a high-level response to persuasive writing.

Your task

Comment on a writer's use of language, showing how well you understand the implications of their word choices.

Approaching the task

Read the text below, which is based on an extract from a website about orangutans, then write answers to the questions that follow.

Orangutans live in the tropical rainforests of Borneo and Sumatra (part of Indonesia and Malaysia). They depend on the forest to survive.

Mining has caused irreversible damage – illegal open cast mining for gold has turned the lush rainforest into a barren and lifeless desert. Illegal logging has also devastated protected areas here, and they are now threatened by another industry.

Indonesia and Malaysia are the world's largest palm oil producers and our demand for this commodity is increasing every year. It is used in many processed foods, including ice cream, chocolate, chips, cereals, frozen foods, margarine, biscuits, cakes, breads and even fruit juice. Increasingly it is marketed as a 'green' biofuel for vehicles. To feed this demand, the tropical rainforest is being destroyed and converted to oil palm plantations, where nothing else can grow.

Fires have also caused terrible destruction to Indonesia's forests and killed, orphaned and displaced many orangutans. A combination of factors – dry debris from logging, use of fire by palm oil companies and a longer than normal dry season – have allowed fire to devastate a huge area. Some campaigning groups have suggested that the fires have been started deliberately to clear the forests.

The Orangutan Foundation protects the orangutan but also recognises that their habitat is unique in its richness of biodiversity and crucial for local communities, who are as dependent on the forest as the orangutan.

Adapted from www.orangutan.org.uk

 1

a) Find a word in paragraph 2 which shows that the harm from mining in the forest cannot be repaired.

b) Find a word in paragraph 4 which shows that the campaign groups cannot prove that fires were started deliberately.

2 Write down the meaning of each of the following words from the extract. Try to use only one word or a short phrase in your definition:

a) devastated

b) commodity

c) unique

d) crucial.

3 Look at the sentence in paragraph 3 beginning, 'Indonesia and Malaysia are the world's largest...' What does this sentence tell the reader?

a) The palm-oil industry is growing every year, even though we do not use much of it.

b) The palm-oil industry is growing every year because Indonesia and Malaysia produce so much of it.

c) Consumers are responsible for the growth of the palm-oil industry because they use so much of the oil.

4 Read paragraph 2 again. How does the writer use language to make the landscape sound uninviting?

Reflecting on your progress

Response 1

1 The writer describes the landscape by using the words **2** barren and lifeless desert This means that mining has made the land dry and dusty. **3**

1 A point introduces the evidence, which uses some words from the question but not all those that are needed.

2 A short, relevant quotation has been used, but there are no quotation marks.

3 The explicit meaning of the quotation has been explained.

Comment on Response 1

This is a good attempt to explain the effects of the language. However, there is no examination of individual words, which makes the explanation too general. The word 'uninviting' from the question has been missed out, which means that it is not clear *how* the landscape has been described.

5 Using the comments above and progress points 1b–3b in the Check your progress section at the end of this chapter, rewrite this response to improve it.

Response 2

3 .4

1 The writer makes the landscape sound uninviting by **2** using the words 'barren and lifeless desert'. This means **3** that mining has made the land dry and dusty. The word **4** 'barren' suggests nothing will ever grow again in this place. Therefore it creates the impression that the landscape is uninviting. **5**

1 This is a clear point that uses the key words from the question.

2 A short, relevant quotation is used correctly, with quotation marks.

3 The explicit meaning of the quotation is explained.

4 This examines what is suggested by an individual word, but it does not explain why.

5 This links the explanation back to the question, but does not explore the reason for the connection or the writer's purpose.

Comment on Response 2

This answer explains the implicit meaning of an individual word and is clearly focused on answering the question. However, it needs to give reasons for the inferences and explore the writer's purpose.

6 Using the comments above and progress points 1c–3c in the Check your progress section at the end of this chapter, rewrite this response to improve it.

Contributing to a group discussion

You will learn how to:
- speak for a particular purpose
- make an effective contribution to a group discussion.

When taking part in a discussion, it is important to make informed comments. To be able to do this, you will need to research your topic carefully and expand on your points when asked about them.

Introducing the skills

Look at these statements for and against zoos:

For	Against
Zoos educate the public.	Animals suffer stress and boredom.
Zoos save endangered species.	There can be overpopulation of some species, due to pressures to breed 'cute' baby animals.
Zoos have breeding programmes.	Some zoos kill their surplus animals.
Visiting a zoo is a family activity.	Zoos teach children that imprisoning animals for entertainment is acceptable.
Seeing a live animal up close is a personal and memorable experience.	Animals suffer ill health and become unfit.

1 Note down two more points that could go in each column of the grid.

2 Read through the four pieces of evidence below, then match each piece of evidence to one of the arguments in the grid.

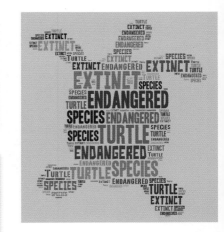

Evidence 1: A study of UK zoos found that 75% of elephants were overweight and only 16% could walk normally, the remainder having various degrees of lameness.

Evidence 2: Tigers and lions have around 18,000 times less space in zoos than they would have in the wild.

Evidence 3: Only 23 amur leopards are left in the wild because of poaching and habitat destruction, and they're only being kept alive because of breeding programmes in zoos.

Evidence 4: At the Saint Louis Zoo, about 400,000 children and adults participate in formal programmes, including classes and Camp KangaZoo each year.

3 Could you match evidence to all of the points? Why do you think a lack of evidence might be a problem during a discussion?

When you take part in a discussion, other members of the group will question you on your points. You need to be able to back up and explain your arguments clearly.

4 How could the following exchange between two students be improved?

Farah: Why do you think that zoos should be closed down, Akeem?

Akeem: I think they should be closed down because animals are locked up and they get bored.

5 Rewrite Akeem's response, adding evidence to support his point. Begin with the phrase, 'For example…'

6 Look at this example discussion topic:

In a group, discuss and answer the question: Should we ban zoos?

Decide what you might need to find out in advance so that you could take part successfully in the discussion. Make a list of points to research.

Developing the skills

In a group discussion, someone needs to act as the **chairperson**. In order to be a good chairperson, you need to have questions ready to ask. You also need to be able to encourage all members of the group to take part.

The following are good leadership skills in a discussion:

- **Initiating:** 'Right, let's get started, do we agree with this statement?'

- **Asking questions:** 'How many zoos have been prosecuted for poor conditions?'

- **Involving others:** 'What do you think, Bill?'

- **Summarising:** 'Going back over what we have all said, it is clear that…'

7 Read the following part of a discussion about zoos. Match the leadership qualities listed above to the things that Lin, the chairperson, says.

Lin: So, are we in favour of zoos or against them, Jenny?

Jenny: Zoos are wrong. They keep animals locked up in cages for our entertainment and that isn't fair.

Lin: Tamas, what do you think?

Tamas: Well, I think zoos can be a force for good because they have breeding programmes for animals.

Jenny: Why is that important?

Tamas: Because breeding programmes stop many endangered animals in the world from becoming extinct.

Lin: So, we have arguments both for and against zoos. On the one hand they could be viewed as confining animals but they have also had a good impact on increasing the population of endangered species.

8 Imagine you have been asked to chair the discussion question above. Answer the following questions to help you prepare:

a) How will you start? For example, will you ask a question to open up the discussion?

b) Will each person speak in turn?

c) How will you make sure that each person makes a full contribution?

d) Why is summarising important?

e) How might you help the group reach a conclusion?

9 In groups of three, discuss the topic 'Should zoos be banned?' One person should chair and the other two should argue the two different points of view. When you have finished your discussion, swap roles and try again.

Applying the skills

10 Work in groups of five. Hold a discussion on the following topic:

Should we ban zoos?

One person should chair the discussion. Two of you should argue *for* banning zoos and the other two should argue *against* banning zoos. At the end of the discussion you must agree on an answer to the question.

Checklist for success:

✔ Take it in turns to present your views.

✔ Listen carefully to each other and do not interrupt.

✔ Use evidence to support your views.

✔ Expand on your answers by explaining your reasons.

✔ Ask questions to clarify and develop ideas.

✔ Summarise the main points of view.

Check your progress:

I can express a viewpoint in a discussion.

I can provide evidence to support my views and explain my reasons in a discussion.

I can support others in a discussion by asking questions, summarising views and taking the initiative.

Using complex sentences to develop ideas

You will learn how to:
- use complex sentences
- rearrange your sentences to create different effects.

Varying sentences can create different effects in argumentative writing – for example, by developing ideas or changing the emphasis of a sentence.

Introducing the skills

Read the text below.

> The zoo has been involved in helping save endangered species for decades. Our goal today is to create a sustainable future for wildlife and people around the world.

This text uses only simple sentences. In order to link and develop arguments effectively, you need to use **complex sentences**:

> While the zoo has been involved in helping save endangered species for decades, our goal today is create a sustainable future for wildlife and for people around the world.
>
> From www.stlzoo.org

Key terms

complex sentence: a sentence that contains a supporting idea (subordinate clause) in addition to the information in the main idea (main clause)

Main idea (main clause).

Comma marks off the extra information.

Supporting idea (subordinate clause).

Linking word.

This sentence shows the link between what the zoo has done in the past (helped save endangered species for decades) and what its goal is now (to create a sustainable future for wildlife and people around the world).

1 Copy these sentences and underline the <u>supporting idea</u> in the sentence.

a) For all the money spent, the life of a zoo animal is no different now.

b) If you are going to the zoo today, I urge you to look closely.

Complex sentences usually use **conjunctions** or **prepositions** to link the supporting idea to the main idea. For example:

although	however	while	when	if	for	all

2 Circle the words that link the ideas in each of the sentences you copied from Question 1.

3 Copy and complete each of these complex sentences using a word from the word bank above.

a) …zoos breed endangered species, many people consider them to be cruel.

b) …you look at a caged tiger, you will see the boredom in his eyes.

Key terms

conjunction: a word used to link clauses in a sentence (e.g. 'and', 'but', 'if')

preposition: a word indicating the relationship of one thing to another (e.g. 'for', 'in', 'by')

Developing the skills

The subordinate clause in a complex sentence can often be put in different places in the sentence. This can change the emphasis of the sentence:

- *Although he was well fed*, the tiger hated the cage.
- The tiger hated the cage *although he was well fed*.

When the subordinate clause is at the start of the sentence, you have to put a comma before the main clause.

4 Rewrite the following sentences, moving the subordinate clause to the end:

a) Even though zoos provide safety and food, many animals suffer from frustration.

b) After many years helping to conserve endangered habitats, the zoo won an environmental award.

Applying the skills

5 Write a paragraph arguing that zoos should be closed down. Ensure you use a range of complex sentences.

Checklist for success:

✔ Use complex sentences to add further detail to one main idea.

✔ Choose the position of the subordinate clause carefully for emphasis.

Check your progress:

I can form complex sentences.

I can create different complex sentences for different effects.

I can use complex sentences to create a wide range of effects.

Structuring an effective argument

You will learn how to:
- use connective phrases to show how ideas are linked
- structure an argument in a clear way.

It is important to signpost your writing, so that the reader can follow the direction of your argument.

Introducing the skills

Read the text below about how important it is to protect endangered species.

Tigers, elephants and orang-utans are beautiful creatures and should be saved from extinction. These animals are dying out because of humans and this is unfair. **1**

Firstly, humans have been destroying the habitats of creatures around the world. For example, orang-utans have been displaced from the forests of Indonesia and Malaysia due to human production of palm oil, illegal open cast mining and illegal logging. Humans are killing orang-utans just so that they can make more money. **2**

Another reason innocent creatures are becoming extinct is due to humans taking animals out of the wild for the **3** exotic pet trade. According to WWF, there are more tigers living in American gardens than in the wild. It is estimated that at least 5,000 tigers are kept captive in the USA, but there are as few as 3,200 tigers left in their natural habitats. This is a shocking statistic that reveals that humans are more concerned with using animals as status symbols, than with protecting them. In addition to this, many of the people who privately own tigers in the USA are not trained to look after animals. Consequently these powerful creatures could be neglected, abused and mishandled.

Some people might argue that species dying out is part of the evolutionary cycle and that is natural for some less successful creatures to become extinct as the world changes around them. **4**

However, this is not the case for the majority of these **5** creatures. There is no evolutionary reason for elephants to become extinct. They are only at risk because of poaching, conflict with humans and habitat loss.

1 The first paragraph outlines the main argument.

2 The second paragraph outlines a way that humans have been helping to kill animals.

3 The third paragraph links to the previous one, using a connective phrase.

4 The fourth paragraph provides new information from a different point of view.

5 The writer rejects the previous information, using a connective phrase.

In conclusion, our world's biodiversity is under threat and **6** we need to do something about it. If we do not take action, then elephants, orang-utans, tigers and many more beautiful creatures will die out. We must act now, or we will lose these endangered species forever.

6 The final paragraph brings together the ideas.

1 Using your own words, sum up the writer's main argument in paragraph 1.

2 Which sentence in paragraph 2 provides evidence to back up the claim that humans have been spoiling habitats?

3 Which word or phrase creates the link between the second and third paragraphs?

4 Which word or phrase in paragraph 4 shows that this point of view is not the writer's?

5 Which phrase in paragraph 5 helps the writer reject the previous idea?

6 How does the writer bring together the ideas in the final paragraph? Which phrase helps to do this?

Top tip

In the sentence containing evidence, notice how the writer has given three examples. This is called the *rule of three* and it is a common technique used by writers to make a point memorable.

The writer has signposted the argument by using key words and phrases to help the reader find their way around the argument.

In the grid below are some helpful signposting words and phrases for the beginning of paragraphs:

Listing	Firstly, secondly... finally... First and foremost... Most importantly...
Introducing the counter-argument	Some people may argue... Admittedly, ... Some might argue that...
Contrasting	On the other hand... However... Never the less... Despite that...
Concluding	In conclusion... To conclude... Overall... To sum up...

Developing the skills

7 Draw up a list of the arguments for and against zoos.

8 Now plan six paragraphs for a piece of argumentative writing either for or against zoos. Copy and complete the grid opposite to help with your planning.

Part of argument	Ideas and evidence	Signposting phrase
1 Introduction • Begin with a statement in which you make your point of view clear. • Provide one clear reason.		
2 Advance your argument • Write a paragraph in support of your argument. • Start with a new point and back it up with evidence such as facts and quotations.		
3 Develop your argument • Write a second paragraph in support of your argument. • Start with a different point and back it up with evidence.		
4 Counter-argument • Write a paragraph that introduces a counter-argument.		
5 Dismiss the counter-argument • Argue against the previous point.		
6 Conclusion • Summarise your points and reinforce your view to the reader.		

Applying the skills

9 Using the plan you created in Question 8, write the argument for paragraph 2 or 3, using signposting phrases to guide the reader through your points.

Checklist for success:

✔ Keep the focus of your paragraph on one fresh idea.

✔ Include evidence (facts, statistics or quotations) to support your idea.

✔ Give reasons for the importance of the evidence.

✔ Use signposting words and phrases to signal the direction of your points.

Check your progress:

I can use signposting words to guide my reader.

I can use connectives to show relationships between my ideas in a series of paragraphs.

I can structure a piece of argumentative writing using connectives, evidence and reasons.

Writing a persuasive letter

You will learn how to:
- combine the persuasive and argumentative writing skills you have learned in one text
- understand what makes a high-level piece of persuasive or argumentative writing.

Your task

Write a letter to a newspaper arguing either for or against keeping animals in zoos.

Approaching the task

1 Plan your ideas. Your plan could take the form of a spider diagram – for example:

They educate the public – help children to understand animal behaviour better.

Save endangered species – able to breed endangered animals and provide a safe haven for them.

Zoos

Animals suffer stress and boredom – but modern zoos have better facilities which enable animals to live in more natural surroundings.

Visiting a zoo is a family activity – provides wholesome entertainment and happy memories for the whole family.

2 Now take your best ideas and order them into a sequence of paragraphs. For example:

Paragraph	Focus on...
1	Main argument that zoos are beneficial for animals and humans.
2	
3	
4	
5	
6	

3 Copy the grid below to remind yourself of the different ways that you can use vocabulary, evidence, paragraphs and sentence structure to create convincing arguments. Tick off each skill or feature as you use it in your draft.

Feature	Done
paragraphs, each with a separate focus	
evidence to support your ideas	
reasons for the importance of your evidence	
signposting words and phrases	
variety of type and length of sentences to develop ideas and create persuasive impact: • simple • compound • complex	
features of argumentative writing • rule of three • interesting adjectives	

4 Come up with a striking opening. For example:

> Visiting zoos as a child is one of my most magical memories. Surely every child deserves the same opportunity to learn about the animal kingdom in this way?

5 Now write your argument. When you have finished, read through your work to check for errors in spelling, punctuation and grammar.

Reflecting on your progress

Response 1

1 Zoos are good for animals. **I** believe that it is important that we support zoos because they help **2** to protect endangered species. The Saint Louis Zoo works with other zoos to make sure that they are able to breed endangered species in the best way **3** possible. This means that animals under threat of extinction will continue to survive. **4**

1 A simple sentence clearly sets out the writer's opinion, but the vocabulary could be more interesting.

2 Justifies the opening statement and uses 'because' to provide a reason.

3 Gives an example.

4 Explains the importance of the evidence.

Comment on Response 1

This is a good attempt at creating an argument, but all the sentences are simple or compound. There is use of evidence and some explanation, but there are not many linking words or phrases used to connect the various points in the argument. The student also does not make good use of many features of argumentative writing. Introducing a few complex sentences and adding more connective words and phrases would make this argument more convincing.

6 Using the comments above and progress points 4b–7b in the Check your progress section at the end of this chapter, rewrite this response to improve it.

Response 2

First and foremost, zoos are good for animals. **1** Although in the past some zoos have mistreated animals, modern zoos provide a vital service in **2** protecting endangered species. For example, the Saint Louis Zoo works with the Association of Zoos **3** and Aquariums to manage their breeding populations, so that the best matches are made for endangered species. As a consequence, animals under threat **4** of extinction will continue to survive. We need to support zoos, to ensure that endangered species are able to breed, grow and succeed. **5**

1 Signposting clearly sets out the writer's opinion in an ordered way, but the vocabulary is still basic (e.g. 'good').

2 Uses a complex sentence to compare the past treatment of animals with that of the present. An interesting adjective ('vital') is used to create a sense of urgency.

3 Gives a precise example, introduced with a signposting phrase.

4 Explains the importance of the evidence.

5 Uses personal pronouns and the rule of three to heighten the persuasive impact of the paragraph, but the vocabulary could be more emotive (e.g. 'flourish').

Comment on Response 2

The argument is clearly signposted and the evidence and reasons are linked effectively using connective words and phrases. There are some good examples of the features of argumentative writing and a range of sentences are used to develop ideas. However, there are still some basic examples of vocabulary. Perhaps using more emotive language would help.

7 Using the comments above and progress points 4c–7c in the Check your progress section at the end of this chapter, rewrite this response to improve it.

Check your progress

1a	I can identify the features of a persuasive text.
2a	I can understand the purpose of a persuasive or argumentative text.
3a	I can support an answer with a quotation, using the correct punctuation.
4a	I can express my views and listen carefully to others in a discussion.
5a	I can form simple, compound and complex sentences.
6a	I can use connectives to link sentences.
7a	I can use occasional evidence to support my argument.

1b	I can recognise the use of positive adjectives in persuasive texts.
2b	I can understand the explicit and implicit meaning of words and phrases.
3b	I can explain the reasons for a writer's choice of vocabulary.
4b	I can express my views in a discussion and provide evidence to support them.
5b	I can form complex sentences to create specific effects.
6b	I can use signposting words to link ideas between paragraphs.
7b	I can use evidence and some reasons to support my argument.

1c	I can identify the features and purpose of persuasive and argumentative texts.
2c	I can explain the explicit and implicit meanings of words and link them to a writer's purpose.
3c	I can explain the effect of quotations, giving reasons for my inferences.
4c	I can give reasons for my own views in a discussion and support others by asking questions.
5c	I can use a variety of different sentence structures to create a range of effects.
6c	I can use a variety of signposting words and phrases to link ideas between sentences.
7c	I can use a variety of evidence and reasons to develop my argument.

Chapter 4
Descriptive writing

What's it all about?

This chapter explores how writers build evocative descriptions of imagined places in science-fiction and fantasy novels and short stories.

You will learn how to:
- analyse how writers use language to describe
- use quotations to support your opinions
- identify different techniques used in descriptive writing
- choose precise vocabulary and imagery
- vary sentence structures for effect
- use paragraphs to organise description.

You will:
- annotate in detail a passage of descriptive writing
- role-play a television interview with an explorer
- write your own description of a fantastical or futuristic place.

What is descriptive writing?

You will learn how to:
- identify key techniques in descriptive writing
- consider the effects of language on descriptive writing.

Descriptive writing is the language that writers use to create pictures, or images, in a reader's mind.

Introducing the skills

A good descriptive writer chooses their words carefully to convey specific ideas.

Read the paragraph below. Important adjectives, nouns, verbs, and adverbs have been highlighted.

> The old man shuffled slowly down the busy street, his feet tired and aching. Making an effort to keep gradually moving, he breathed heavily. Confused, he looked around blankly as his pale eyes searched for something he might recognise. He lowered his head, fixed his attention on the ground and, blinking away tears, continued on his slow, desperate journey.

1 Discuss how each word class has helped to describe the man.

2 How might different word choices change the meaning of the description? For example, what would be the effect of changing the verb and adverb 'shuffled slowly' to 'walked briskly'?

Developing the skills

Writers also build up their descriptions through imagery – using words to create a picture in the reader's mind. There are three main types of imagery: **simile**, **metaphor** and **personification**.

Key terms

simile: a comparison between two things that uses the words 'as' or 'like' (e.g. 'My dad sleeps *like* a bear in hibernation')

metaphor: a type of comparison that describes one thing as if it is something else (e.g. 'In winter, my dad *is* a bear in hibernation')

personification: when an object is described as if it has human characteristics

3 Read the paragraph below and identify the examples of simile, metaphor and personification.

> The trees in the forest rose from the ground like green skyscrapers. Their branches linked hands and embraced to create a dense canopy of leaves and flowers. A sweet scent poured from flowers of every imaginable colour whilst bees buzzed between the petals, drinking their nectar.

4 What does each technique add to your impression of the setting? Copy and complete the framework below to help you write your ideas as full sentences.

> In the description, the simile '…' suggests how … the trees are.
>
> The branches are described using '…' and the phrase '…' makes them sound as if …
>
> The author also uses metaphor when he writes '…' and this helps the reader to imagine …

Applying the skills

5 Copy out and annotate the extract below, picking out the vocabulary and imagery that create a powerful description of a cave.

> The children stepped into the mouth of the cave and were swallowed up by the darkness. Turning on their torches they could see stalactites descending from the roof of the cave like huge teeth. Water dripped down through the darkness, tapping and echoing on the stone below, or splashing coldly on their skin. Filled with terror, they continued inside. In the weak torchlight, shadows flickered threateningly along the walls of the cave. Something whispered through the blackness.

6 What other descriptive techniques has the writer used to describe the setting?

7 Choose three of the techniques you have identified and write a paragraph explaining what each one describes and the effect it creates for the reader.

Check your progress:

I can identify some types of descriptive words.

I can identify and use different descriptive words and techniques and consider their effect on the reader.

I can recognise and use a range of descriptive words and techniques to achieve specific effects in my writing.

Using quotations from descriptive writing effectively

You will learn how to:
- select information from a text to support your points
- explain why writers make different language choices.

When writing about a descriptive text, you need to select quotations (the actual words and phrases used by the writer) and think about how the writer uses them to put ideas across to the reader.

Introducing the skills

Read the extract below.

> The twins gasped.
>
> Above them, at the top of a sparkling staircase that spiralled up into the canopy of the forest, sat an enormous glass sphere, the size of St Paul's Cathedral. The surface reflected the glittering black sky. It must have been attached to the trees but gave the impression of being magically suspended, as if by a spell.
>
> 'Is that really where the Dark Princess lives?' asked Orphea, but her brother wasn't listening. He had already stepped onto the staircase in his excitement.
>
> 'Wait for me!' she called, and raced after him, the two of them climbing up like tiny ants.

1 Are the following statements true or false?

a) This part of the story takes place in the daytime.

b) The twins are impressed by their first sight of the sphere.

c) The sphere looks small.

d) The staircase is grimy.

e) The children are made to feel small next to the sphere.

2 Find quotations from the text as evidence for each of your answers to Question 1. For example, you could prove that a) is false by quoting: 'glittering black sky'.

Developing the skills

Once you have chosen a quotation, you need to explain why it specifically shows that you have a strong answer. For example, if you had written 'This part of the story takes place at night, as it mentions "glittering black sky", you could add: 'The adjectives "glittering" and "black" suggest it is night-time.'

3 Add a specific comment about how each quotation provides evidence for your answers to statements b–e in Question 1.

Applying the skills

4 Read the extract below and decide whether you would describe the **atmosphere** as happy or miserable. Select the words that suggest this to you and write a paragraph explaining why.

> Everything seemed dead. The grey trees stood motionless as the dusty, polluted air swirled around them. No birds sang from their branches. The ground was thickly carpeted with ash, grey and **contaminated**, with no sign of any blade of grass. The man hopelessly searched the barren landscape: he was utterly alone.

Key terms

atmosphere: the main mood or emotions in a piece of writing

Vocabulary

contaminated: poisoned or polluted

Check your progress:

I can select some words and phrases from a text that show what setting or atmosphere is like.

I can select a range of words and phrases from a text that show what setting or atmosphere is like.

I can select a range of words and phrases, and begin to explain what they reveal about setting and atmosphere.

Explaining how writers use different descriptive techniques

You will learn how to:
- explain how writers use different techniques to convey meaning
- structure explanations clearly.

When writing about a text, you need to comment on the different techniques of language and structure the writer has used to get their ideas across to the reader.

Introducing the skills

As well as using vocabulary and imagery, writers make use of sounds, repetition and different sentence types to help the reader picture the scene being described.

Read the extract below.

> The police patrol ship whirred through the air as it checked on the servants living in the apartment blocks. Each of the vast, steel buildings held one thousand apartments, and each apartment was fronted by a huge glass window so the servants could be monitored easily. It was past curfew time and anyone not asleep would be arrested and punished. Violently. Everything was silent except for the low rumble of the patrol ship's engine. Everyone had learned, past 8pm, to stay in bed, their eyes closed, their breathing slow, hoping they looked asleep.

Descriptive writing

1 Copy and complete the grid. Use the definition of each technique to help you find an example in the text.

Technique	Definition	Example
repetition	using a word more than once to highlight its importance	
list	a sentence that contains several linked images in order to build up an idea	
short sentence	a sentence that gets across an important idea without using many words	
onomatopoeia	a word that sounds similar to the actual sound it is describing	

2 The text imagines a futuristic city where there are many strict rules and everybody is scared. How does the writer use repetition, short sentences, lists and onomatopoeia to convey this sense of unfairness and fear? Write a sentence on each of these techniques. For example:

> The patrol ship is presented as frightening through the word 'rumble', which uses onomatopoeia to link the police to something threatening like thunder.

Developing the skills

It can be difficult to explain how a writer uses descriptive features to get across their ideas. It helps to follow a simple structure for your explanation:

- State a clear idea about what the writer has done in the text.
- Support your idea with a quotation as evidence.
- Explain how specific features of your quotation are used by the writer.

Read the following extract. The highlighted sections show how the writer has tried to create a harsh, wintry setting and develop an atmosphere of fear.

Ser Waymar looked him over with open disapproval. 'I am not going back to Castle Black a failure on my first ranging. We will find these men.' He glanced around. 'Up the tree. Be quick about it. Look for a fire.'

Will turned away, wordless. There was no use to argue. The wind was moving. It cut right through him. He went to the tree, a vaulting grey-green **sentinel**, and began to climb. Soon his hands were sticky with sap, and he was lost among the needles. Fear filled his gut like a meal he could not digest...

Down below, the lordling called out suddenly, 'Who goes there?' Will heard uncertainty in the challenge. He stopped climbing; he listened; he watched.

The woods gave answer: the rustle of leaves, the icy rush of the stream, a distant hoot of a snow owl.

The Others made no sound.

Will saw movement from the corner of his eye. Pale shapes gliding through the wood. He turned his head, glimpsed a white shadow in the darkness. Then it was gone. Branches stirred gently in the wind, scratching at one another with wooden fingers. Will opened his mouth to call down a warning, and the words seemed to freeze in his throat. Perhaps he was wrong. Perhaps it had only been a bird, a reflection on the snow, some trick of the moonlight. What had he seen, after all?

'Will, where are you?' Ser Waymar called up. 'Can you see anything?' He was turning in a slow circle, suddenly wary, his sword in hand. He must have felt them, as Will felt them. There was nothing to see. 'Answer me! Why is it so cold?'

It was cold. Shivering, Will clung more tightly to his perch. His face pressed hard against the trunk of the sentinel. He could feel the sweet, sticky sap on his cheek.

A shadow emerged from the dark of the wood.

From *A Game of Thrones* by George R.R. Martin

Vocabulary

sentinel: a person or thing that watches (often on guard and from high up)

Metaphor: the comparison makes the wind seem dangerous.

Adverb: 'suddenly' makes the reader feel how on edge the characters must be.

Onomatopoeia: the sound helps the reader imagine the setting. It is eerily quiet and the sudden noise of the bird might scare Will.

Rhetorical question: Will is questioning his surroundings; he is anxious and feels in danger.

Key terms

rhetorical question: a question that is used to make people think, rather than expecting an answer

3 Read the four completed annotations. Now identify and write an annotation for each of the other features and techniques highlighted in yellow that you have learned about in this chapter so far.

Applying the skills

4 Look back at your annotations from Question 3. Choose your three best ideas and write them up into three clear, concise paragraphs that explain how the author has created a harsh, wintry setting with an atmosphere of fear. For example:

> The writer uses Will's behaviour to create a sense of fear, 'he listened; he watched'. The two verbs include different senses and show that Will is alert and worried. This suggests to the reader that there is danger in the forest.

Check your progress:

I can find some different techniques that writers use in descriptive writing.

I can identify different descriptive techniques and begin to explain why and how the writer has used them.

I can select a range of descriptive techniques and explain why and how the writer has used them.

Checklist for success:

✔ Identify a language feature in the description, such as repetition or onomatopoeia, and explain its effect.

✔ Select a quotation from the description.

Responding to descriptive texts

You will learn how to:
- combine the reading skills you have learned when responding to a descriptive text
- understand what makes a high-level response to descriptive writing.

Your task

Explore the ways that the writer creates an interesting setting and builds up a negative atmosphere in the extract below.

Approaching the task

Read the extract. It is set in London in the year 2300, when the city has been devastated by conflict. This passage focuses on a girl's arrival in the suburbs of the city and her description of how it looks.

> Home was once a kingdom of toppling towers, of flaking concrete, shattered glass and brick dust underfoot. There were flooded towers, great ruined houses, ancient stone buildings with no roofs. The floors of churches a thousand years old had stone flags slippery with **algae**.
>
> That was then.
>
> And this was now: flat, green and low. An open **acreage** of crippled **suburbs**. The wide acres of brick houses, detached and semi-detached, estate after estate of them opening out on either side of the crumbling roads that used to be Finchley. The walls would stand for centuries, but the roofs of most had long gone. Many of the old houses were now factories, shops and offices. The gardens **enclosed** by the old housing estates had been cleared and the fences knocked down to form fields. Beyond the houses, on the fringes of the city, were the big fields that grew seven-eighths of the fresh food for the enclosed city, acres of beans and potatoes and cabbages and leeks.

Vocabulary

algae: a simple, water-dwelling plant

acreage: area of land

suburbs: residential areas around a city

enclosed: closed off on all sides

cannibalised: broken down and reused

vermin: animals that are pests and carry disease

No one travelled far these days. Petrol was a luxury for the rich. Buses and trains lay rusting in the street, every useful part **cannibalised** decades ago. The bus stations had been turned into cowsheds. The tunnels where the Northern Line trains once ran were a home for rats, mice and other **vermin** – thieves, for instance, or beggars sheltering from the rain. And prisoners. The prisoners of London kept prisoners of their own. Lifetimes had been spent trapped in these filthy, damp passages.

From *Bloodtide* by Melvin Burgess

Key terms

narrator: the character telling the story in the first person

1 Complete these tasks, exploring different ways in which the extract creates an interesting setting and builds up a negative atmosphere.

a) This extract focuses on what the **narrator** can see. Make a list of the nouns that she uses to describe the landscape.

b) What type of objects does she concentrate on? Why do you think she does this?

c) Find two adjectives that are used to describe the area as it used to be and two as it is now.

d) What effect do these words have on you?

e) What kinds of people and animals are described in the extract?

f) What is the effect of these choices?

Top tip

Remember that a writer wants to:

• create questions in your mind so that you read on

• help you to imagine that you are there by stimulating your senses

• help you understand the characters' feelings.

2 Based on your answers to Question 1, pick out two features of the text that make the setting interesting *and* two features of the text that create a negative atmosphere.

3 Now write each point as a clear paragraph. Use the following sentence starters for help:

> One way in which the setting is made interesting is by describing...
>
> The author also creates a negative atmosphere in the setting when describing...

Reflecting on your progress

Response 1

1 One way in which the author creates a negative atmosphere is by describing the houses as, 'a kingdom of toppling **2** towers'. By saying this he makes them sound as if they are dangerous. **3**

1 Makes a clear point linking to the question.

2 Includes a relevant quotation.

3 Explains the effect of the description.

Comment on Response 1

This response attempts to explain how description has been used to create a negative atmosphere. It begins with a clear idea and supports it with a relevant quotation. However, the explanation would be better if it focused on the effect of a specific word or technique.

4 Using the comments above and progress points 1b–3b in the Check your progress section at the end of this chapter, rewrite this response to improve it.

Response 2

1 One way in which the author creates an interesting and negative atmosphere is by describing the buildings as, 'a **2** kingdom of toppling towers'. The word 'toppling' suggests **3** that the buildings look wild and aggressive, as if they are going to fall down. This suggests that they are unstable **4** and perhaps have been damaged by something, which makes the reader wonder what has happened to the city.

1 Clear point linking to the question.

2 Includes a relevant quotation.

3 Explanation of the effect of a technique.

4 Development of explanation by looking at the effect on the reader and explaining how it is created.

Comment on Response 2

This is a good response, making a clear point, related to the question, and using a relevant quotation. The effect of the quotation is explained with reference to a technique, and then the explanation is developed further.

5 Using the comments above and progress points 1c–3c in the Check your progress section at the end of this chapter, rewrite this response to improve it.

Varying descriptive vocabulary

You will learn how to:
- use vocabulary imaginatively
- use imagery to build up descriptions.

Try to use interesting and imaginative vocabulary in your descriptive writing. If you always use the simplest and most obvious words, you will not create a precise picture for your reader.

Introducing the skills

Read this description. A time traveller to the future is having a meal with some robots.

> I sat down at the long table and began to eat the green cubes of jelly they placed on my dish. I took a bite and was amazed. They were really good! I really liked the taste. They had a taste a bit like curry.
>
> 'I really like these little cubes. What is in them?' I said to the robot next to me.
>
> 'Humans,' it said.

1 Which words give a clear and precise description of the meal?

2 Which words or phrases are not very clear or are repeated?

What could you do to improve this description? Firstly, you could use synonyms to avoid having the same word twice.

3 Find the places in the text where you could use the following synonyms:

a) flavour

b) adore.

Secondly, you could choose more precise words or phrases to help your reader build up a clear picture. In the text, the writer uses the phrases 'really good' and 'a bit like curry'. Neither of these descriptions tells us very much.

4 Which *two* of these more precise words would have been better?

delicious disgusting bland tasteless yummy spicy

There is one final word that is repeated and is not as precise as it should be – 'said'.

5 Think of two alternatives for the word 'said' that could be used in the text.

6 Once you have considered all these changes, rewrite the text in full, with all the new vocabulary in place.

Developing the skills

Practise what you have learned with these short exercises.

7 Choose the most precise or accurate adjective for each of the following sentences, then write them out:

   a) There were deep puddles of a silvery liquid that I had to splash through, so I got completely (damp/wet/soaked/moist).

   b) I was so fed up with my journey that I didn't notice the (enormous/big/large/plump) robot towering over me as I approached.

   c) 'Stop, human!' he thundered in a (loud/gentle/deafening/soft) voice.

8 Replace the repeated verbs in this paragraph with alternatives from the word bank:

The gigantic robot looked at me angrily as if I were a small ant. Then he looked closely at my face and the expression on his face changed. A kindly smile crossed his ugly lips. He picked me up, as if I was a feather, and looked at my clothing, hair and the equipment I carried in detail.

'You're harmless,' he said, and put me down.

glared	stared	peered	peeped
inspected	glimpsed	glanced	saw

> **Top tip**
>
> It can help to use a dictionary to check the precise meaning of a synonym, to make sure that the word fits your sentence.

9 Now draft a paragraph in which you describe an unfriendly robot attacking the friendly robot. Use as many specific verbs as you can. You could start like this:

> Suddenly, another robot appeared as if from nowhere. It had a face like a dented tin can. 'Do not let the human into the city!' it cried. The friendly robot raised its arm and...

10 When you have finished, swap paragraphs with a partner and ask them to check you have used the most suitable, powerful verbs.

Imagery can help you to create pictures in the reader's mind. Two useful types of imagery are similes and metaphors.

11 Identify the images in the sentences below, then say whether each image is a simile or metaphor.

a) The unfriendly robot gave off a smell like an overheated engine as he staggered around.

b) I shrank back, spluttering like a fish out of water.

c) The injured robot tottered over me, a grey and green mountain about to topple over.

d) I ran for my life, haring along the path back to the spacecraft.

12 Your images should always be appropriate. Look at this sentence:

> The robot strode along the path like a tiny ballerina.

a) What is wrong with the image in this sentence?

b) Think of an alternative image that would be more appropriate.

13 Choose the most appropriate simile or metaphor for each of these examples:

a) The robot strode along the path like a lumbering elephant/a curious cat/a frightened gazelle.

b) The spaceship buzzed and hovered above me like a clumsy hippo/an enormous moth/a graceful swallow.

c) Gratefully, I raced up the platform into the ship's curly hair/gaping mouth/floppy ear.

You should always give as much detail as possible in your descriptions. To help you plan this detail, you can use a spider diagram. Look at this example:

From this, you might then write:

> The cave was as dark as a deep, dank well. Faint rays of moonlight crept through the narrow entrance, casting pools of light onto the floor. The darkness crowded in on me, pressing against my skin and making me terrified.

14 Create a spider diagram to help you describe a bright control room on a spacecraft.

Applying the skills

15 Write at least one paragraph about the control room in your spacecraft.

Checklist for success:

✔ Use precise vocabulary and try not to repeat verbs or adjectives.

✔ Create some interesting similes or metaphors to bring your descriptions to life.

Check your progress:

I can choose some specific adjectives and verbs for my descriptions.

I can use a variety of vocabulary and some imagery to create interesting descriptions.

I can use a range of precise vocabulary and imagery to create interesting descriptions.

Varying sentences in descriptive writing

You will learn how to:
- use different sentence structures
- vary your sentence lengths and structures for effect.

Varying your sentences can create different effects in your imaginative writing – for example, by changing the pace or introducing sudden surprises.

Introducing the skills

Read the following descriptive text:

> The surface of the island was very flat. The air was silent. I stepped out of the hovercraft. I took a pace. I immediately leapt back. The ground was freezing. I needed some special shoes. I retreated into the craft.

1 There is some good description here, but what do you notice about the sentences?

2 How could this text be improved?

Simple sentences

All the sentences in the description above are *simple*. Simple sentences have a subject and a verb. They normally tell us about one thing or action.

I stepped out of the craft. — subject / verb

Compound sentences

To vary your sentence lengths, you can link two simple sentences to create a *compound* sentence. A compound sentence is made up of two equal sentences joined using one of the following conjunctions:

or	and	but	so	yet	nor

I stepped out of the craft and looked around me. — subject / verb

3 Turn these simple sentences into compound sentences using one of the conjunctions from the word bank above:

a) The monster's eyes suddenly half-opened. He didn't see me.

b) I crept up to the treasure chest. I lifted the lid.

c) I knew I had to be quick. The monster would spot me.

To link similar ideas or events, you can turn several simple sentences into one longer compound sentence:

> I stepped out of the hovercraft. I took a pace. I immediately leapt back.
>
> ⬇
>
> I stepped out of the hovercraft, took a pace and immediately leapt back.

These actions are linked, so you do not need to repeat the subject 'I'.

However, you do need to add a comma between the first two actions.

Finally include the conjunction 'and' before the final action.

4 Turn each set of separate sentences into one connected sequence of actions:

a) Our captain walked ahead. He stopped. He consulted his digi-map.

b) The skies turned grey. They filled with snow. They released it in a huge shower.

c) I groped for a rock. I grabbed something. I screamed out in fear.

5 Now look at this paragraph by another student:

> Our spaceship weaved through the meteorite storm, sped through another cluster of stars and hovered above our destination. It was the wrong city.

Copy the paragraph and underline the sequence of linked actions. Then circle the simple sentence that tells you something new or surprising.

Complex sentences

A complex sentence contains one main idea. It is usually a simple sentence with extra detail added to it. Complex sentences often use conjunctions such as:

> even though   although   because   while   whenever   where

> We decided to land our spacecraft in the city, — main idea
> — a comma marks off the extra information
> even though we were lost and worried. — supporting idea
> — linking phrase

In this example, the main idea could be a sentence on its own because it has a subject and a main verb. The supporting idea and linking words would not make sense on their own.

6 Copy these sentences and underline the main idea that could be a sentence on its own. Remember – it may not come at the start of the sentence.

a) Even though we were starving, we thought it was dangerous to stop to eat.

b) We decided to seek shelter in an abandoned building, before night came.

c) The whole city was silent, although it did not feel at all safe.

7 Copy these complex sentences, then fill in the gaps with conjunctions.

a) …our captain was out on patrol, a strange light appeared outside.

b) We grabbed our kit and left by the back exit, …it was now bitterly cold.

c) …we called the captain on his portaphone, we got no reply.

Good descriptive writing uses different types of sentence to create different effects. Read this extract from a novel:

> The great sentinel was right there at the top of the ridge, where Will had known it would be, its lowest branches a bare foot off the ground. Will slid in underneath, flat on his belly in the snow and the mud, and looked down on the empty clearing below. His heart stopped in his chest.
>
> From *A Game of Thrones* by George R.R. Martin

8 a) Pick out the complex sentence that tells the reader about a particular object and then adds supporting information.

b) Find the compound sentence that shows two equally important actions taken by the main character.

c) Find the simple sentence that shows Will's surprise.

In the extract, you may have noticed how commas are used to separate out an additional detail.

9 Identify the 'additional' information in these three sentences:

a) Suddenly a voice came over the portaphone, distant and crackly, so we stopped and listened hard.

b) I pressed the portaphone as close to my ear as I could, the cold steel against my cheek, but I couldn't make anything out.

10 What extra information is given in each case?

Applying the skills

11 Imagine you are one of the crew in the abandoned city of the future. Your captain has gone missing and you are now in charge. At first you see no signs of life, but then you notice a strange glow coming from a skyscraper. You decide to investigate…

Write a paragraph describing your entry into the skyscraper.

Checklist for success:

✔ Join linked actions together into one sentence using commas and the conjunction 'and'.

✔ Use compound sentences for information that is related or equally important.

✔ Use complex sentences to add further detail to one main idea.

✔ Use commas to mark off additional information.

✔ Use simple sentences for shock or surprise.

Check your progress:

I can form some different sentence structures.

I can use some different sentence structures to create specific effects.

I can use a variety of different sentence structures to create a wide range of effects.

Using paragraphs constructively

You will learn how to:
- use paragraphs to build detail in descriptive writing
- use a range of prepositions to clarify descriptions.

Paragraphs will help you organise information when you are describing different aspects of a setting or experience.

Introducing the skills

Read these three paragraphs from a novel called *The First Men in the Moon*. The narrator and his companion are lost and cannot find their spacecraft ('the sphere'). Suddenly, they hear a sound...

> I stared about me in the vain hope of recognising some knoll or shrub that had been near the sphere. But everywhere was a confusing sameness, everywhere the [...] bushes, the [...] fungi, the [...] snow banks [...]. The sun scorched and stung, the faintness of an unaccountable hunger mingled with our **infinite perplexity**. And even as we stood there, confused and lost [...], we became aware for the first time of a sound upon the moon other than the air of the growing plants, the faint sighing of the wind, or those that we ourselves had made.
>
> Boom... Boom... Boom.
>
> It came from beneath our feet, a sound in the earth. We seemed to hear it with our feet as much as with our ears. Its dull **resonance** was muffled by distance [...]. No sound that I can imagine could have astonished us more, or have changed more completely the quality of things about us. For this sound, rich, slow, and deliberate, seemed to us as though it could be nothing but the striking of some gigantic buried clock.
>
> From *The First Men in the Moon* by H.G. Wells

Vocabulary

infinite perplexity: confusion that does not end

resonance: sound

1 The first paragraph begins by describing the narrator's confusion. What *new* information comes in the final sentence of the paragraph?

2 What does the short second paragraph tell the reader?

3 How is the third paragraph linked to the first and second paragraphs?

The writer has used each paragraph for a different reason:

- The first paragraph gives the reader an *overall picture* of the scene and the characters' feelings.

- The second paragraph *surprises* the reader with the sound. The shortness of the paragraph emphasises the sound.

4 What does the narrator tell the reader about the scene in general in the first paragraph?

5 What other details about the sound can you find in the third paragraph?

Now look at this picture of a futuristic city:

6 Create a spider diagram to plan out all the things that you could describe in this scene.

[ ]

[ ]

Futuristic city

[ ]

Dark blue sky

[ ]

Dome-shaped building

[ ]

7 Now plan four paragraphs of a piece of writing that describes your own arrival in this city.

Your first paragraph should be a general description of the scene.

Add ideas for the next three paragraphs. Use a table like the one below to help with your planning.

Paragraph	Focus on...
1) the general scene (a description of the city as a whole)	the sky, the sun, the bullet-like building, the skyscrapers
2) the fierce sun	its glare, the bright blue sky, its reflections, it blinds us…
3)	
4)	

Developing the skills

How you organise ideas *within* your paragraphs is also important. You can use prepositions to make sure your reader is really clear about where an event takes place or where something is positioned.

In the extract from *The First Men in the Moon*, the writer says that the sound 'came from beneath our feet'. Here, 'beneath' tells the reader the location of the sound.

Other common prepositions to do with location are as follows:

on	around	upon	above	behind
below	between	inside	under	

8 Copy this paragraph, then fill in the gaps using appropriate prepositions from the list above.

> ...our heads, a huge metallic bird soared. It held a silver worm...its claws and, after circling...for several minutes, it landed... a metal platform near where we stood. There was a nest...the platform made of iron bolts, old spanners and nails. ...the nest we could just make out three thin-necked chicks.

9 Now write your own paragraph describing this strange metallic bird feeding its chicks. Try to use at least three different prepositions. Use these prompts to help you:

a) The strange bird placed its feet...

b) It opened its mouth and...

c) Then it flew...

Applying the skills

10 Go back to the plan you made in Question 7. Choose one paragraph and write your description. It can be your opening paragraph that sets the scene or one of the later, more focused paragraphs.

Check your progress:

I can plan paragraphs that each have a different focus.

I can plan and use paragraphs for different effects.

I can plan and use paragraphs for a range of effects and use prepositions for precision.

Checklist for success:

✔ Keep the focus of your paragraph on one aspect or idea, but include lots of detail about it.

✔ Use prepositions to give precise information about the location or position of whatever it is you describe.

Writing descriptively

You will learn how to:
- combine the descriptive writing skills you have learned in one text
- understand what makes a high-level piece of descriptive writing.

Your task

Describe a landscape or city from the future. You can base it on the image in Topic 7 or on the one below. Or you can imagine your own futuristic landscape or city.

Approaching the task

1 Plan your ideas. Your plan could take the form of a flow diagram or a spider diagram like this:

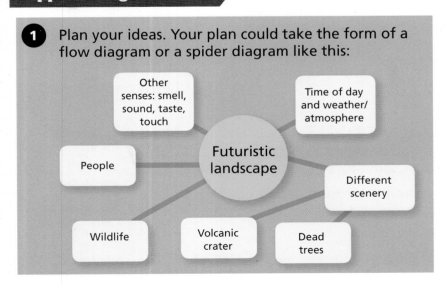

2 Now take your best ideas and put them into a sequence of paragraphs. For example:

Paragraph	Focus on...
1	time of day/weather/atmosphere
2	dead trees
3	
4	

Top tip

As this is description, you do not need lots of action or speech.

3 Copy the table below to remind yourself of the different ways in which you can use vocabulary, imagery, paragraphs and sentence structure to create imaginative and engaging descriptive work. Tick off each skill or feature as you use it in your draft.

Feature	✔
Paragraphs each with a separate focus	
Different lengths of paragraphs for effect	
Prepositions to indicate the position and location of things and people	
Variety of type and length of sentences to create surprise, add detail or show a sequence: <ul><li>simple ('The tree was dead.')</li><li>compound ('The tree was dead and the wind howled.')</li><li>complex ('The tree was dead, although something stirred in the branches.')</li></ul>	
Precise vocabulary (do not repeat adjectives or verbs unnecessarily)	
Use of imagery: similes that use 'like' or 'as' and metaphors	

4 Come up with a striking opening sentence. For example:

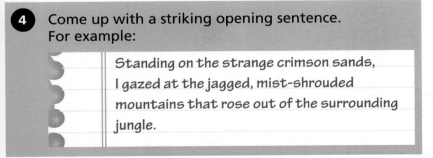

Standing on the strange crimson sands, I gazed at the jagged, mist-shrouded mountains that rose out of the surrounding jungle.

5 Now write your description. When you have finished, spend five minutes reading through your work and checking for any errors in spelling, punctuation and grammar.

Reflecting on your progress

Response 1

1 I woke up with my face in the sand. The sand was red
2 as I looked around me. I could see a big jungle and a
big path. There were mountains that disapeared into **3**
the clouds. I walk into the jungle and it was massive. **4**
5 The trees were like rockets. The leaves were as big
as plates and the flowers were enormus. They were
brightly coloured. Reds and blues and greens and **6**
purples they looked like nothing I had ever seen before.

1 Quite an interesting short opening sentence.

2 Use of details but vocabulary could be more interesting.

3 Third and fourth sentences could be combined using a comma and 'and'.

4 A new paragraph could be used to show the change of location. The description changes from past to present tense; it should stay the same.

5 Two good similes and some good adjectives. Some spelling mistakes with more complex words.

6 Punctuation needs improving here as the last sentence does not make sense. The colours could be added to the previous sentence to form a list.

Comment on Response 1

This is a good attempt at creating a description, but all the sentences used are simple or compound. Using a wider vocabulary and introducing a few complex sentences to develop descriptions would bring the scene to life. The student should use a new paragraph every time a new idea or new aspect of the scene is introduced.

6 Using the comments above and progress points 4b–6b in the Check your progress section at the end of this chapter, rewrite this response to improve it.

Response 2

[1] In the city of the future, hundreds of cars were whizzing through the air. **[2]** The dull grey metal and thick black exaust **[7]** fumes almost stopped the sunlight reaching the streets beneath. Horns were constantly sounding from impatient drivers as they rose and dived through the busy skys. **[7]** **[3]**

[4] The dark streets below were just as packed. Even though the metal pavements moved and glided past shops **[5]** and offices, people stood on them quite comfortably. The front of every building was a huge video screen and flashed up constant adverts.

[6] Loud electronic music filled the air like thunder, pouring out of speakers on every street corner. It was deafening.

1	A good opening, with some descriptive detail and sound.
2	Precise, detailed vocabulary to describe the senses and use of the preposition 'beneath'.
3	Paragraph deals with one main idea – the cars.
4	Short sentence and new paragraph changes location to the streets.
5	Complex sentence adds detail.
6	Simile is okay, but a little unimaginative.
7	Some spelling mistakes with unusual words: 'exhaust' has a silent 'h', and sky is a y-plural so should end in 'ies'.

Comment on Response 2

Paragraphs are clearly used for each new idea, but most sentences are the same length. There is some good description using the senses, but very little imagery. Perhaps some use of metaphor would help.

7 Using the comments above and progress points 4c–6c in the Check your progress section at the end of this chapter, rewrite this response to improve it.

Check your progress

1a I can identify some techniques of descriptive writing.

2a I can select some words and phrases from a text that show what setting or atmosphere is like.

3a I can structure a simple explanation.

4a I can choose some imaginative adjectives and verbs for my descriptions.

5a I can use some different sentence structures in my descriptions.

6a I can plan paragraphs that each have a different focus in descriptive texts.

1b I can identify and use a range of descriptive words for particular effects.

2b I can select a range of words and phrases from a text that show what setting or atmosphere is like.

3b I can describe some of the techniques writers use to convey meaning.

4b I can choose words and some imagery to create engaging descriptions.

5b I can choose sentence structure for particular effects.

6b I can plan and use paragraphs for different effects.

1c I can identify techniques in descriptive writing and describe the effects they have on the reader.

2c I can select a range of words and phrases, and begin to explain how they show what setting or atmosphere is like.

3c I can structure a clear explanation about how writers use different techniques to convey meaning.

4c I can use a variety of words and imagery to create interesting descriptions.

5c I can use a range of sentence lengths and structures to create a variety of effects.

6c I can plan and use paragraphs for a range of effects and use prepositions for precision.

Chapter 5
Narrative writing

What's it all about?

This chapter develops the skills needed to understand and write narrative texts. It looks at a range of texts loosely linked to the theme of mystery and suspense, and uses them to explore how writers plan and structure stories to keep the reader engaged.

You will learn how to:

- recognise and explain the features of narrative texts
- identify how writers create and communicate ideas
- create characters and settings
- demonstrate your understanding of story structure
- plan and structure your writing
- punctuate speech
- analyse sentence structure.

You will:

- perform a role-play in character
- review and recommend a narrative text
- write a short mystery story.

What is narrative writing?

You will learn how to:
- understand features of narrative and non-narrative texts
- explore how narrative texts can be structured.

Texts can give us information in many different ways. Some tell stories to communicate a particular idea. These are *narrative texts*. Some writers present information without using a story or characters in *non-narrative texts*.

Introducing the skills

Narrative texts have a **plot**, characters and usually a narrator – the 'voice' that describes the events that take place. A story has a particular **setting** and is usually structured to show how actions and emotions develop over time.

In contrast, writers of non-narrative texts often use features such as lists, graphs and tables to help the reader understand their meaning.

1 Copy and complete the following table to identify whether the types of text in the left-hand column are narrative or non-narrative texts.

Text	Narrative or non-narrative text?
dictionary	
novel	
encyclopedia	
newspaper article	
short story	
autobiography	
recipe book	

Key terms

plot: the events that make up a story and how they relate to one another

setting: where and when a story takes place

Developing the skills

Read the extract below.

> The letter that changed her world was lying on the mat in the hall when she got up for her daily run.
>
> For a moment, Charlotte stared at the spidery black handwriting spelling out her name. Then, she picked it up and placed it on the wooden stand by the hallway mirror. She needed to think. In the reflection, she saw herself: the cropped, almost boyish hair, now dyed black; the slim nose with the diamond stud; the grey-green eyes, deep-set and difficult to read. She hardly even recognised herself since they'd changed her identity and given her a new life, so how could someone know her real name and where she now lived? Should she still go for her run? Now she wasn't sure. She needed to keep up her fitness and keep toned for the job they'd given her. Running, along with kick-boxing, kept her on her toes – literally. But the letter had thrown her.

2 How does Charlotte feel about seeing the letter?

Writers often use a **story arc** to structure narrative texts. This includes a beginning, a middle and an end. At the start of a story, you find out about the main characters and their situations. There may be mysteries that make you want to find out more. Narrative texts also tell you about the time and place in which they are set.

3 Which sentences suggest that the extract above comes from the beginning of a story?

4 Which details from the extract show you that it is set in the present day rather than the past?

5 Which details tell you what *sort* of story it is likely to be?

Key terms

story arc: a continuing storyline with rising tension and excitement in the middle

Applying the skills

6 Summarise the extract using the following headings:

  a) What you learn about the character

  b) What you learn about the situation and setting

  c) How you know this is the beginning of a story

  d) The mysteries that are set up in these first paragraphs

Check your progress:

I can distinguish between narrative and non-narrative texts.

I can explain the main features of narrative texts.

I understand the features of narrative openings.

Identifying how writers communicate ideas in stories

You will learn how to:

- identify the main ideas, themes and purposes of a text
- comment on the writer's use of specific words.

Story writers choose their words carefully to communicate their ideas and make the purpose of their writing clear.

Introducing the skills

 1 If you described this house to make it seem sinister and threatening, what adjectives could you use?

Read this description. Two child evacuees have arrived at the house where they will be staying until the war has ended.

Cecily looked at the house, and held her little brother's hand tightly. There was dark green, almost black, ivy growing over the front door, which had once been white in colour, but was now a pale, faded yellow, eaten up by woodworm. She felt that if she knocked on it, the whole thing would disintegrate into a pile of dust. The whole building looked like a wedding cake that had been left to go mouldy for centuries.

'Not like it,' said Toby, pulling his sister's hand as if to leave.

'We don't have any choice,' said Cecily, as much to herself as to three year old Toby.

Suddenly, Cecily noticed a tatty piece of paper, tucked under the rusty door-knocker. She took it down, and unfolded it.

'Back at three. Wait by door. Ethel Peabody.'

Cecily sighed. What kind of person went out just as two young children, travelling from hundreds of miles away, arrived at their door?

From *The House in the Woods* by Mike Gould

2 Which of these statements reflects Cecily's view of Ethel Peabody's house?

a) It is welcoming and friendly.

b) It is mysterious and exciting.

c) It is unpleasant and unwelcoming.

3 Which words tell you about Cecily's view?

Developing the skills

Writers can tell a story using different narrative **viewpoints**: the **first person** or the **third person**. In this extract, Cecily's story is told in the third person. The writer uses Cecily's viewpoint to describe what Ethel Peabody's house looks like, and to create **tension** and **suspense** in the story.

4 Look again at the final two sentences of the extract. The writer has used a question, from Cecily's viewpoint, to create suspense in the story. What kind of woman do you think Ethel Peabody will turn out to be?

Applying the skills

Now read this description of Ethel Peabody.

From a distance, she looked like a thin, black stork. She was wearing a dusty black dress, and had a long, stretched neck in which a lump in her throat bobbed up and down like a stuck marble. Every now and then she used her umbrella to swipe at any sparrows who had the nerve to look for crumbs on the withered lawn.

From *The House in the Woods* by Mike Gould

5 Write three sentences about the kind of things Miss Peabody might do in the story. For each one, include a quotation from the extract as evidence.

Checklist for success:

✔ Use your own words to describe Miss Peabody's character.

✔ Choose words and phrases from the extract that support your ideas effectively.

Creating characters

You will learn how to:
- develop characters in your own writing
- provide detail about contrasting characters through word choice.

When writing a narrative text, you can give your reader hints about a character or setting by choosing specific words to describe them.

Introducing the skills

1 Look at the picture. If you were describing this boy to make him seem brave and strong, what adjectives would you use?

Read this description of a different teenage boy.

> Eragon was fifteen, less than a year from manhood. Dark eyebrows rested above his intense brown eyes. His clothes were worn from work. A hunting knife with a bone handle was sheathed at his belt, and a buckskin tube protected his yew bow from the mist. He carried a wood-frame pack.
>
> From *Eragon* by Christopher Paolini

2 Who do you find out about in this paragraph? What do you discover about Eragon's age, appearance and character?

3 'Dark eyebrows rested above his intense brown eyes.' What features or qualities does this description suggest about the boy's character?

Developing the skills

Writers can reveal more about a character by showing how they behave when they are with other characters. This adds depth and detail.

4 Read the following extract from the same book. Here, the boy Eragon meets an adult called Sloan. How do the two characters get along? Note down all the the words that show their feelings and reactions to each other.

He had never liked Sloan. The butcher always treated him with **disdain**, as if he were something unclean. A widower, Sloan seemed to care for only one person – his daughter, Katrina, on whom he **doted**.

'I'm amazed,' said Sloan with **affected** astonishment. He turned his back on Eragon to scrape something off the wall. 'And that's your reason for coming here?'

'Yes,' admitted Eragon uncomfortably.

From *Eragon* by Christopher Paolini

Vocabulary

disdain: looking down on someone

doted: cared for and protected

affected: put on

5 Look back at the list of adjectives you used to describe the boy in Question 1. Write a list of the *opposites* of the words you have used. For example, if you said the boy was 'brave', the opposite would be 'cowardly'. If you said he was 'strong', the opposite would be 'weak'. Include contrasting words for his physical appearance as well as his character.

6 Use the two lists you have created to describe two contrasting characters. Write three phrases about your two characters. For example:

> The boy was brave and strong. The man was cowardly and weak.

Applying the skills

7 Write a paragraph about a meeting between two contrasting characters. Choose your words carefully to make the differences between them clear. You could start like this:

> The door slammed behind the boy and he turned to face…

Checklist for success:

- ✔ Like the writer of *Eragon*, use suitable words to tell your reader about the characters.
- ✔ Use appropriate adjectives and verbs to create detail.
- ✔ Use a mixture of short and long sentences to include action and description.

Check your progress:

I can describe characters using adjectives.

I can use different adjectives to describe contrasting characters.

I can describe contrasting characters and show the relationship between them.

Creating settings

You will learn how to:
- comment on a writer's use of language to create setting
- comment on settings that tell readers about mood and character.

In narrative texts, writers often use settings to tell their readers something about the story and the characters in it. They also use descriptions of the setting to create the mood or atmosphere of the story.

Introducing the skills

1 Look at the words in the word bank below. Which ones would you choose to create a setting that is beautiful and calm?

gleaming   soft   rocky   peaceful   rough   pearly   dark

2 Look at the picture of a forest. What words and phrases would you use to describe this forest if you wanted to present it as mysterious and frightening?

Read this extract. A boy, Eragon, is approaching a city that he has never seen before.

He found himself standing on a granite outcropping, more than a hundred feet above a purple-**hued** lake, brilliant under the eastern sun. The water reached from mountain to mountain, filling the valley's end. From the lake's far side, the river flowed north, winding between the peaks until – in the far distance – it rushed out onto the eastern plains.

To his right, the mountains were bare, save for a few trails, but to his left...to his left was the dwarf city. Here the dwarves had reworked the seemingly **immutable** rocks into a series of **terraces**. The lower terraces were mainly farms – dark curves of land waiting to be planted – dotted with **squat** halls, which as best he could tell were built entirely of stone. Above those empty levels rose tier upon tier of interlocking buildings until they **culminated** in a giant dome of gold and white. It was as if the entire city was nothing more than a line of steps leading to the dome. The **cupola** glistened like a polished moonstone, a milky bead floating atop a pyramid of gray slate.

From *Eragon* by Christopher Paolini

Vocabulary

hued: coloured

immutable: fixed and rigid

terrace: flat area

squat: short and wide

culminated: finished or topped

cupola: dome

3 What is the mood as the boy approaches the city? How do you think he feels as he views this landscape?

4 Which words and phrases are most effective in creating this mood? Copy and complete the grid below, adding two more examples of each word type.

Nouns	Verbs	Adjectives
'outcropping'	'he found himself'	'purple-hued'

Developing the skills

Writers also use settings to reveal things about what kind of person a character is.

Read the extract below. Cecily and her brother are exploring Ethel Peabody's garden.

> The lawn, if that was the right word, was a series of ashy mounds and dusty patches, through which the odd blade of sickly grass peeped. It was surrounded by huge, overgrown hedges each with the look of an octopus trying to suck the life out of the soil with their twisted tentacles. Here and there, dotted about the remains of the grass, were numerous rusty old rabbit traps, some, sad to say, containing the bleached skeletons of the desperate creatures who had dared to set foot on the lawn, many years back.
>
> From *The House in the Woods* by Mike Gould

5 What kind of character is suggested by a house with a garden containing so many animal traps? Choose an adjective from the list and explain your choice. Think about the kind of reaction many people have to snakes.

mysterious   suspicious   friendly   gentle

6 Do you think the house owner will turn out to be a kind and welcoming character?

Applying the skills

Read the extract below. A young woman is approaching a house, searching for someone she used to know. However, the house is not what she expected it to be.

I proceeded: at last my way opened, the trees thinned a little; presently I beheld a railing, then the house – **scarce**, by this dim light, distinguishable from the trees; so **dank** and green were its decaying walls. Entering a **portal**, fastened only by a latch, I stood amidst a space of enclosed ground, from which the wood swept away in a semicircle. There were no flowers, no garden-beds; only a broad gravel-walk girdling a **grass-plat**, and this set in the heavy frame of the forest. The house presented two pointed **gables** in its front; the windows were **latticed** and narrow: the front door was narrow too, one step led up to it. The whole looked, as the host of the Rochester Arms had said, 'quite a **desolate** spot.' It was as still as a church on a week-day: the pattering rain on the forest leaves was the only sound **audible** in its **vicinage**.

'Can there be life here?' I asked.

From *Jane Eyre* by Charlotte Brontë

Vocabulary

scarce: hardly

dank: wet and rotten

portal: gateway

grass-plat: lawn

gables: triangular part of a wall near the roof of a building

latticed: small window-panes

desolate: lonely and unloved

audible: able to be heard

vicinage: nearby area

7 Write a paragraph explaining how the writer describes this setting. Consider:

- what the reader learns about the house and garden
- the words that describe the setting
- what the narrator finds unusual about the house and garden
- how the setting reveals what the character is feeling
- what the setting suggests about the person who lives there.

Checklist for success:

✔ Choose two or three parts of the extract to write about.

✔ Include particular words and phrases from the extract to comment on.

✔ Explain how setting and the character's mood are linked.

Check your progress:

I can recognise words that create setting.

I can understand how adjectives create character through description of setting.

I can comment on how setting reveals a character's mood.

Understanding story structure

You will learn how to:
- explain features of narrative texts
- understand how readers choose which texts they like.

Stories are structured to get the reader interested and involved. They usually include a series of problems and difficulties that are resolved by the end.

Introducing the skills

Many narrative texts with a story arc have a three-part structure: a beginning, a middle and an end:

- At the beginning, the reader learns about the characters and the situation they are in.

- In the middle, the characters encounter problems or obstacles that must be overcome, and tension or excitement increases.

- At the end, the problems are solved and the characters' goals are achieved.

Writers plan their stories carefully, considering the goal they want their characters to achieve and the difficulties that might stop them achieving it too easily. For example, many children's stories end with the sentence, 'They all lived happily ever after', but the characters have to overcome many difficulties before they reach this happy ending.

1 Think of a story you have read where the characters must overcome a series of difficulties before reaching a happy ending. For example, you might think of a fairy tale such as *Sleeping Beauty*. Write down these problems and obstacles.

2 Imagine you are going to write a story called 'The Treasure Hunt'. Which of these events would be obstacles to the hero or heroine finding the treasure?

a) They lose the treasure map.

b) They find digging tools.

c) The weather is perfectly calm.

d) They are captured by thieves.

e) The key does not fit the treasure chest.

Developing the skills

Readers usually choose stories that have the kind of end goals they like. For example, a reader might like a romance that ends happily, an action story in which the hero saves the day or a detective story in which a crime is solved.

3 What type of end goals interest you? Write a list. Which **genres** of story include these end goals?

Applying the skills

4 Think of another story you have read and enjoyed in which the characters face several obstacles. Draw a timeline of events that shows the starting point, the obstacles that the characters face in the order they appear, and the end goal. For example:

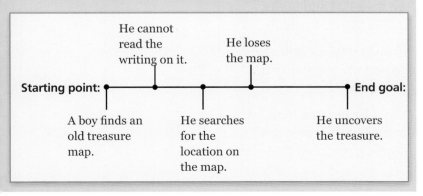

Key term

genre: a type of text – stories in the same genre usually have similar features; genres include science fiction, romance, adventure and horror

Check your progress:

I can explain why readers choose particular types of writing.

I can plan a story based on an end goal.

I can structure a story with obstacles and an end goal.

Responding to narrative texts

You will learn how to:
- combine the reading skills you have learned when responding to narrative texts
- understand what makes a high-level response to narrative writing.

Your task

Write a short review for your class, explaining what a novel extract is about and giving reasons why your fellow students should read it.

Approaching the task

Read the extract below. It is about a boy who kicks a football over a church wall and when he goes to find it, he ends up in a magical world. At this point in the story, he has just entered a mysterious castle.

> The first room was an **armoury**, lined with racks, which held a few swords, **pikes**, and shields. It took up the whole width of the keep.
>
> Roland drew a sword from one of the racks. The blade was sharp, and well greased. And that was another strange thing about the castle. Although it was a ruin, the scars were fresh. The tumbled stone was **unweathered** and all the windows held traces of glass.
>
> He replaced the sword: it was too heavy to be of use.
>
> Roland continued up the stairs to the next door. He opened it and looked into a barren room. Shreds of tapestry hung against the walls like skeletons of leaves, and there was one high window of three lancets [...] and the glass of the middle **lancet** was scattered on the floor [...] and in the hearth opposite the window lay a white plastic football.
>
> Roland took the ball between his hands, just as he had pulled it from under the lorry. The pattern of stitches: the smear of oil and brick dust: it was the same.
>
> He stared at the ball, and as he stared he heard a man singing. He could not hear the words, but the voice was young, and the tune filled Roland with a yearning that was both pain and gladness in one.

Where's it coming from? he thought. The next room up?

If only he could hear the words. Whoever was singing, he had to hear. But as he moved, the voice stopped.

'No,' whispered Roland.

The ball was dropped from his fingers, and for a long time he listened to its slow bounce – bounce – bounce – down – and round – until that was lost.

'He must be up there.'

Roland started to climb. He came to the room above; the last room, for ahead the curve of the stairs grew brighter as it opened on to the top of the **keep**.

There was no one in the room. But under the window stood a low, white, marble table, and draped from one end, as though it had been jerked off, was a tapestry of cloth of gold. Roland went to the table. It was quite plain, except for the shape of a sword cut deep in the stone. He picked up the golden tapestry and spread it over the table. It dropped with the folds of long, untouched use, and the impression of the sword was in the cloth.

From *Elidor* by Alan Garner

Vocabulary

armoury: a room for storing weapons and armour

pike: a long, pole-shaped weapon

unweathered: not marked by the weather

lancet: a narrow window that comes to a point at the top

keep: a tower built inside a castle

1 What does the following quotation tell you about the castle?

> Although it was a ruin, the scars were fresh. The tumbled stone was unweathered and all the windows held traces of glass.

2 Find a quotation from the extract which shows that Roland is nervous about what he might experience in the castle.

3 Why do you think the writer uses the following simile to describe the wall hangings?

> Shreds of tapestry hung against the walls like skeletons of leaves.

4 What questions does the extract raise that make you want to know more?

5 Now write your review of the extract. Use the following headings to structure your writing in three paragraphs:

- Explanation of the extract
- The way that the castle's appearance and contents are described
- How the writer creates suspense and makes the reader want to know more

Aim to use some of the key terms you have met in this chapter, such as narrative, viewpoint, structure and suspense.

Reflecting on your progress

Read the following responses to the task. Look at the annotations and think about how each response could be improved.

Response 1

> In this book a boy goes inside a castle to look for his ball. The castle is scary. It says 'that was another **1** strange thing'. This makes me think that the castle is weird and I wonder what will happen next. **2**

1 Uses words or phrases from the extract to support the point.

2 Simple attempt at explaining how suspense is created in the extract.

Comment on Response 1

Although this response shows some understanding of the text and the way it builds tension, it could be improved by giving a bit more detail at all points and by considering the way in which the extract has been written.

6 Using the comments above and progress points 1b–5b in the Check your progress section at the end of this chapter, rewrite this response to improve it.

Response 2

1 This extract is from a narrative which tells a story of a boy exploring a magical castle. The story is told from the viewpoint of the boy. To describe the castle, the writer uses interesting words such as **2** 'strange' and there is also a simile 'like skeletons of leaves'. This makes the reader feel that the castle **3** is mysterious, but also could be dangerous. **4** The story made me want to read on because we do not know who is singing or where the missing sword has gone or what might be done with it.

1 Recognises the type of text and uses the correct word to describe it.

2 Uses a selection of evidence from the story, but does not really explain why these words are interesting.

3 Identifies how suspense is created.

4 Explains the details used to engage the reader in the story.

Comment on Response 2

This response shows a good understanding of the structure of the extract and how it develops and creates suspense. Suitable short quotations are chosen to show how the writer engages the reader, although it would be better if the student explained exactly how these create mystery. The response is particularly good at explaining why a reader would want to read on.

7 Using the comments above and progress points 1c–5c in the Check your progress section at the end of this chapter, rewrite this response to improve it.

Speaking in character

You will learn how to:
- create a character's voice to explore texts
- show your understanding of characters and ideas through role-play.

You can develop your understanding of characters and the part they play in a story by using role-play to put yourself in their place.

Introducing the skills

Remind yourself of the characters of Cecily and Miss Peabody. Read this extract from later on in the narrative.

> 'Where is Toby?' demanded Cecily, rushing into the sitting-room. 'I haven't seen him all day!'
>
> At first, Ethel Peabody didn't answer but instead stabbed the non-existent fire with a long poker. The fire gave up the ghost and went out, with a puff or two of smoke.
>
> 'If your brother had been more respectful, then...'
>
> 'What have you done with him?' cried Cecily.
>
> 'Little children are best not seen or heard,' she replied, stiffly – pointing in the direction of the hallway.
>
> Cecily rushed out, and pulled open the door under the stairs. Switching on the pale lamp, she raced down the rickety stairs to the damp, sour-smelling cellar. As she did so, something large and hairy scuttled across her path.
>
> There in the middle of the cellar stood her brother on a stool, his mouth open in a silent scream. All around him, a blanket of rats tumbled and fell over each other as they tried to mount the legs of the stool to get at the quivering figure above. Grabbing a broom from the nearby wall, Cecily charged furiously into the room scattering the rats as she went. She swept Toby up and ran from the cellar, up the stairs and into the hallway. They were safe.
>
> From *The House in the Woods* by Mike Gould

 1 Imagine that you are Cecily. Write a list of adjectives to describe your thoughts and feelings.

Developing the skills

When exploring a character in role, it is effective to use a structure similar to a narrative text.

2 Consider Cecily's thoughts and feelings, before, during and after she sees her brother.

Thoughts and feelings before seeing her brother	
During	
After	

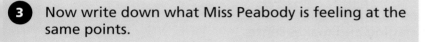

3 Now write down what Miss Peabody is feeling at the same points.

Applying the skills

4 Use the adjectives relating to thoughts and feelings you have noted to prepare a short speech about this incident in role either as Cecily or as Miss Peabody. Imagine you are speaking to yourself.

   a) Think about how Ethel says, 'Little children are best not seen or heard'.

   b) Think about how Cecily says, 'What have you done with him?'

   c) Aim to recreate these tones of voice in your role-play.

Checklist for success:

✔ Prepare two paragraphs (enough for 30 seconds of speech).

✔ Use your understanding of character to explore Cecily's thoughts and feelings.

✔ Structure your speech with a beginning, a middle and an end.

Check your progress:

I can create a character's voice in role.

I can use detail to develop a character's voice.

I can create narrative and character using detail when in role.

Planning narrative writing

You will learn how to:
- plan and organise your writing
- convey your ideas through effective organisation and sequencing.

Planning your narrative text is important in creating a clear structure for your reader. Planning properly will also help you develop and build the reader's interest in the plot by creating exciting obstacles and end goals.

Introducing the skills

1 Imagine you are writing a mystery story and have lots of great ideas. You need to put them in order to ensure your narrative is engaging and makes sense. Copy out these plot points in the order you would place them within a story arc:

a) A boy discovers an underground cave.

b) A boy notices that people are disappearing from his town.

c) Police track a boy by his phone to the cave.

d) A boy is captured and placed with other children.

e) A group of children are rescued.

f) A boy follows kidnappers to the cave and phones the police.

Before you start writing a story, you should note down your ideas for the plot. You could write these as a simple list, or write the title in the middle of the page then note your plot ideas around it as a spider diagram.

2 Create a spider diagram with some ideas for a story called 'A Most Mysterious Day'. For example:

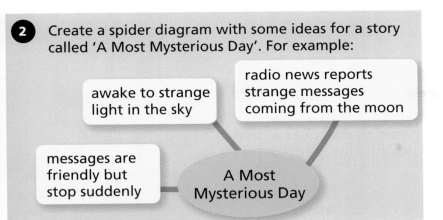

Developing the skills

The next stage when planning a story is to *organise* your ideas. There are three main categories to consider:

- **Plot:** What happens in the story? What is the end goal of your story? What obstacles must be overcome to reach it?

- **Character:** Who is involved in the story? What are they like? What are their relationships with one another? It is best to have just two or three main characters.

- **Setting:** Where does the story take place? What does this place look like? Where is it in space and time?

3 Make a list of setting and character points, adding them to your existing spider diagram. For example:

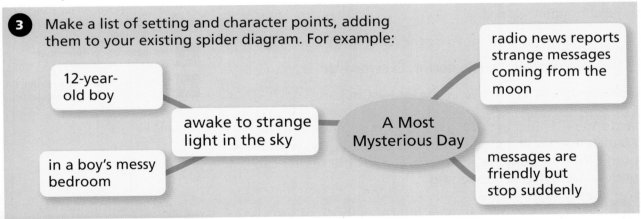

Applying the skills

4 Imagine you are pitching your short mystery story to a magazine. Give a spoken presentation to the editors of the magazine (your class):

- Explain clearly why they should publish your story.

- Present the elements of your plan that readers will find interesting and engaging.

- Be prepared to answer questions from your class.

Check your progress:

I can plan a story using a spider diagram.

I can plan a story, dividing my ideas into characters, setting and plot.

I can generate and shape my ideas in different ways and convey them clearly.

Punctuating speech in narrative

You will learn how to:
- use punctuation to make meaning clear.

Using accurate punctuation when writing **dialogue** helps to make your meaning clear and makes sure the reader knows which character is speaking.

Introducing the skills

Read the extract below.

> **1** 'You'll pay, Jimmy Coates,' seethed the younger man. His accent was a polished English.
>
> **2** 'Who are you?' Jimmy shot back. 'And what do you think I owe you?' **3**
>
> **4** Before they could answer, the door opened, and in burst Georgie, with Felix's mother close behind.
>
> 'Oh!' Georgie shrieked. Jimmy was startled to see a huge smile on her face. 'How's Eva? Is she here?'
>
> 'Eva?' Jimmy gasped.
>
> 'Eva?' gasped the two men on the floor. 'Eva's dead.' **5**
>
> Jimmy stared at them in horror. Everybody froze.
>
> From *Jimmy Coates: Revenge* by Joe Craig

Key terms

dialogue: a conversation between two or more people in a piece of writing

1 The first word inside speech marks always begins with a capital letter.

2 Speech from different characters goes on a new line.

3 Speech always begins and ends with punctuation – here, the writer uses a question mark to show Jimmy's confusion and lack of knowledge.

4 An exclamation shows that Georgie is surprised.

5 A short sentence ending with a full stop emphasises this information.

Four characters are speaking in this passage. The writer has used different punctuation marks so that the reader can understand what is happening.

1 Which punctuation mark indicates shock or surprise?

2 Which punctuation mark shows confusion?

Top tip

Question marks, exclamation marks, commas and full stops tell you how a character is saying a sentence and show you their feelings. If they are confused, they might ask a question. If they are angry or excited, they will make an exclamation.

Developing the skills

3 What are the feelings of the main characters in this extract? How do you know? Write a paragraph describing the feelings of these characters and explaining how the writer shows this.

Applying the skills

The extract below is the next section of dialogue from the same story. The punctuation has been left out.

> Jimmy didn't kill anybody Georgie said quickly And especially not Eva Why would he do that She's taking a massive risk to help us
>
> Hey Jimmy shouted to his sister Careful what you say. We don't know who these men are yet
>
> Of course we do Georgie replied This is Quinn and Rick – Eva's brothers
>
> From *Jimmy Coates: Revenge* by Joe Craig

4 Copy out the passage, adding the correct punctuation to show:

   a) where the speech begins and ends

   b) what the characters feel.

Check your progress:

I can use some punctuation in dialogue.

I can use punctuation to show when different characters are speaking.

I can use a range of punctuation marks to make it clear how characters feel.

Structuring narrative writing

You will learn how to:
- organise your writing using paragraphs and connectives
- create characters with a specific voice.

You can control the pace of a story by using paragraphs of different lengths. You can also use connectives to clarify the order of events and show how they are linked. Useful connectives to show time and order include:

> then   now   afterwards   shortly   when   soon   next

Introducing the skills

Long paragraphs often add detail, while shorter paragraphs can be used to present action.

Read this extract from a narrative text:

> CRASH!
>
> Something slammed into Jimmy's back. The wind was knocked out of him. He fell forward and smacked his chin against the wall. He tasted blood, but didn't have time to do anything about it. As soon as he hit the wall, he spun off it again. Just in time – a fist plunged down at him, aiming a knife at exactly the point where the back of his neck had been. The blade scraped across the tiles.
>
> Jimmy looked up to see two intruders. Both were covered head to toe in black. Their faces were obscured by balaclavas with tiny slits cut for their eyes. The one furthest from Jimmy pushed the bathroom door shut. Then he flicked on a torch and shone it right in Jimmy's eyes.
>
> 'Is that him?' he whispered.
>
> 'That's him.'
>
> Their voices were muffled by their headgear and in any case, Jimmy didn't have time to analyse how they sounded. The closer man raised his fist above his head. A sliver of moonlight outlined his knife. There was nowhere for Jimmy to go. The bathroom was barely big enough for one person – let alone three.
>
> From *Jimmy Coates: Revenge* by Joe Craig

1 What genre do you think this text belongs to? Which words and phrases tell you this?

2 Look at the paragraphs in the extract. Copy and complete the grid below to explain what happens in each paragraph.

Paragraph	What happens?
1	Something hits Jimmy hard
2	
3	
4	
5	
6	

Developing the skills

You can change the voice and viewpoint from which a story is told. The extract above is written in the third person ('he'). This means that the reader sees the action from Jimmy's perspective, but without being 'inside' his head.

3 Rewrite the following sentences in the first person, as if Jimmy is telling the story himself:

> Something slammed into Jimmy's back. The wind was knocked out of him. He fell forward and smacked his chin against the wall.

4 How does this change the mood and tone of the story?

Applying the skills

5 Change the extract so it is written from the perspective of one of the attackers. Use paragraphs to present description and action. Use connectives to show how actions are linked. Write in the first person ('I').

Check your progress:

I can use connectives to show how events are linked.

I can use long paragraphs to add detail and short paragraphs to present action.

I can create characters using the first-person and third-person voice.

Writing a suspenseful narrative

You will learn how to:
- combine the narrative writing skills you have learned in one text
- understand what makes a high-level piece of narrative writing.

Your task

Write a short story that contains suspense and mystery. The title of the story is 'The Stolen Parcel'. Use all the skills that you have built up in this section: planning your writing, punctuating speech, structuring your writing and creating characters.

Approaching the task

Planning what you will write and then sticking to your plan will give your story a good structure and make sure it is interesting to read.

1 Come up with some ideas for story beginnings. What do the words 'mystery' and 'suspense' mean to you? You could look these words up in a dictionary, or online, to give you some starting ideas.

2 Note down all the words, images and ideas that you think of. These could be inspired by other stories you have read or by films you have watched.

3 Now add ideas about the 'stolen parcel' and make connections to mystery and suspense.

4 Draw a spider diagram with your favourite ideas. Use lines to connect ideas and show how your plan is developing.

5 Organise your ideas into three categories: characters, setting and plot. Look back to the list and spider diagrams in Topic 5.8 for help if you need to.

6 Construct a timeline showing the main events in your story. Remember to include at least one event for each part of the story:

  a) Introduce the main character and one problem or mystery.

  b) Include a big problem or catastrophe for the main character.

  c) Explain how the character will resolve the problem or solve the mystery.

7 Write your first draft. Follow your plan closely, making sure that your story is well structured and that the plot makes sense.

8 When you have finished your draft, check it to see if you can make any improvements. Ask yourself these questions:

a) Have I used a range of long and short paragraphs to offer descriptive detail and plenty of action?

b) Is the story written in the first or third person? Have I kept to this throughout?

c) Have I used suitable adjectives and verbs to create characters?

d) Have I used a range of sentence lengths and openings?

e) Have I included dialogue and punctuated the speech to make it clear?

f) Have I used questions to give the reader clues about what will happen next?

Reflecting on your progress

Read the following responses to the task. They are from different points in a story. Look at the annotations and think about how each response could be improved.

Response 1

Nasim lived in a small town. He knew a lot of the people who lived in the town. When he was walking around he **1** would say hello to them. 'Hello,' he would call to the **2** **3** butcher. 'Hello,' he calls to his teacher.

One day, Nasim noticed that there were fewer people for him to say hello to. He only saw one or two of his friends. **4** He wondered if everyone was at home. Perhaps they had all gone on holiday.

However, day after day, Nasim saw only one or two people. It seemed as though people were gradually **5** disappearing, and his town was becoming more and more empty. Nasim decided that he would have to **6** find out what was happening to all of his friends. He would investigate the mystery.

1 This would be a good place to use a different word to avoid becoming repetitive.

2 An exclamation mark could be used here to show that Nasim is feeling happy and light-hearted.

3 Change from the past to the present tense is incorrect.

4 Another short, simple sentence – more variety of sentence types and lengths is needed.

5 Compound sentence adds more detail.

6 A hint is given about what might happen in the rest of the story.

Comment on Response 1

This response sets the scene and establishes a character to a certain point. However, the text could be made more interesting by using some longer sentences to add detail about Nasim's character. There are hints of suspense, but this could be improved by using short sentences more dramatically and effectively.

9 Using the comments above and progress points 6b–9b in the Check your progress section at the end of this chapter, rewrite this response to improve it.

Response 2

Nasim shifted in his sleep, and gradually woke up. His **[1]** brown eyes opened slowly, as he started to realise what **[2]** had woken him. His brown eyebrows furrowed and wrinkled **[3]** as the full meaning of what was happening sank in.

[4] There were people in his house.

They were moving around, and speaking very quietly, but they had **[5]** woken him anyway, and now he was alert and ready for action.

[6] Nasim got out of bed and went over to his bedroom door. **[7]** He listened carefully at the door. He could hear the men speaking in the hallway.

[8] 'Do you know which room the boy's in?' one of the men hissed.

'Must be the one at the end of the passage. I'll go in first.'

Nasim tensed as he heard this. He thought hard about what he should do. He only had a few seconds to come to a decision. He had to think of the right thing, otherwise he would disappear as well.

1 Descriptive detail gives the reader a clear picture of the character.

2 Longer sentences are used to add detail and description.

3 Suspense is created as the reader does not know what has happened.

4 A single sentence as a paragraph is used to create impact, although the effect could be improved by using more interesting words and an exclamation mark.

5 The reader knows that something is about to happen.

6 More interesting verbs could have been chosen here: 'sprang' and 'tiptoed', for example.

7 Using a different sentence opening would help here.

8 Use of speech, a question and a descriptive verb make a good, dramatic sentence.

Comment on Response 2

A range of sentence lengths are used to keep the reader's interest in this narrative, but a wider variety of sentence openings could improve this further. Dialogue is used well, helping to create suspense and descriptive vocabulary is also well chosen to add detail to character and action.

10 Using the comments above and progress points 6c–9c in the Check your progress section at the end of this chapter, rewrite this response to improve it.

Check your progress

1a I can recognise some features of narrative and non-narrative texts.

2a I can identify the main ideas in a narrative text.

3a I can choose adjectives to describe a character.

4a I can identify words that establish setting in a text.

5a I can explain the types of writing I like and why.

6a I can use my imagination to think about what a character might be feeling.

7a I can plan a simple narrative text.

8a I can use some punctuation when writing dialogue.

9a I can use connectives effectively in narrative writing.

1b I can explain the main features of narrative texts.

2b I can identify the main ideas and the words that create characters in a text.

3b I can choose interesting words to describe different characters.

4b I can show how a writer's word choice creates a particular mood and setting.

5b I can plan a story based on an end goal.

6b I can write and perform in role based on a character in a narrative.

7b I can clearly organise my ideas for a story.

8b I can use punctuation in dialogue to show how a character feels.

9b I can structure a narrative text using long and short sentences.

1c I can identify the features of narrative and non-narrative texts and understand how they can be structured.

2c I can comment on a range of features that writers use to create suspense and to establish characters and settings.

3c I can create vivid characters and show the relationships between them.

4c I can comment on the relationship between mood, setting and character.

5c I can plan a story with a series of obstacles to be overcome and an end goal for my characters.

6c I can use role-play to develop my understanding of a character.

7c I can plan and sequence my ideas for a story so that they are clear and effective.

8c I can use punctuation effectively to show when characters are speaking and how they feel.

9c I can use a variety of sentences types and connectives in a narrative.

Chapter 6

Writing to analyse and compare

What's it all about?

This chapter explores the skills readers need to analyse, review and compare a variety of texts. It looks at a range of poetry and drama texts, and analyses aspects of their structure and style. It also explores how to compare the way in which different texts deal with the same topic.

You will learn how to:

- recognise some of the key features of texts that analyse
- identify the differences between plays and stories
- use speaking and listening skills to analyse
- analyse a poem's shape, sound and structure
- use quotations and connective words to analyse
- compare two texts on the same theme.

You will:

- turn part of a story into a play script
- work as part of a group on a brief given by a film director
- write a comparison of two poems.

How do I analyse a text?

What does it mean to analyse something? When detectives or scientists analyse something, they inspect it, or look very closely at it. This means they find particular details that are interesting or important. From these details they draw conclusions.

Introducing the skills

Have you ever been to see a play or dramatic performance? What can you remember about it? What did you think of it? You probably do not recall everything, but some things may have stuck in your mind – how a character made you laugh, perhaps, or the beautiful costumes.

A student called Lia has been to see a play. Read her **review** of it, written for her school magazine:

Key term

review: a written report of a play, film, video game, album, etc. which gives the writer's opinion

---

The school's production of 'Beauty and the Beast' was magnificent. It has been on for five nights, and every night has been sold out. I went to the final performance and loved every minute of it.

Everything about the production worked well, especially Paolo as 'Beast' and Rita as 'Belle'. Paolo really frightened us! They spoke clearly and with real emotion, and everyone gave a big 'Ahhhh!' when they kissed at the end.

But I want to talk about the wonderful set design. At the back of the stage, there was a shimmering golden staircase. This was part of the Beast's palace. But it was really clever because the staircase turned round and became a huge tree in the forest. When Belle's father was lost, wolves tried to climb it to grab him.

The costumes were also very eye-catching. Beast was not dressed as the usual 'hairy monster' but surprised us all by appearing more like a lizard or dragon; he had horrible green scales and a long tail. Belle was dressed very simply in a white dress with a crimson cape and hood. This made her seem very delicate and fragile, and reminded me of Little Red Riding Hood.

I could go on about all the other students who took part, the teachers who helped and the melodious singing, but there are just too many people to mention! Congratulations to everyone who took part or was involved in the production.

The point of a review is to give your opinion about the performance you have seen.

1 What play did Lia watch?

a) Little Red Riding Hood

b) Beauty and the Beast

c) Dragonslayer.

2 What is Lia's overall view of it? She...

a) loved it

b) hated it

c) thought it was okay.

3 In pairs, discuss your answer to Question 2. How did you know? What words and phrases from the review revealed Lia's opinion?

When you analyse or review, you focus in on particular things. For example, in the first paragraph Lia deals with the success of the play ('every night has been sold out'). She also tells us her general view ('magnificent'). In the next paragraphs, she focuses on particular things she liked about the play and tells us why.

 4   Copy and complete the grid below.

Paragraph	Focus (if any)	Comment/analysis	Evidence
2	The acting of Paolo and Rita.	Lia thought it was good that the audience could hear their words. She thought Paolo was very believable as a monster.	'spoke clearly and with real emotion' 'really frightened us'
3	The set design, in particular the staircase.		
4	The costumes, in particular those of…		
5	None – she is summing up what she feels.		

In the same way that Lia analyses the production of *Beauty and the Beast*, you could analyse *her* review using the evidence you have gathered. One way to do this is to use quotations, choosing particular words and phrases from the text to support the point you want to make.

Read two student responses to Lia's review.

Student A

Lia's review is really positive about the costumes – in fact she really loved them as they stood out so much.

Student B

Lia thought the costumes were very effective. She called them 'eye-catching' and also mentioned how the audience were 'surprised' by the Beast and how he looked. In particular, she liked the Beast's…

5 Which student gives evidence for their view in the form of quotations? Which of Lia's *actual words* from the text has the student selected?

6 Copy and complete the final sentence of Student B's response using one of these phrases:

   a) 'white dress with a crimson cape and hood'

   b) 'melodious singing'

   c) 'horrible green scales and a long tail'.

Applying the skills

7 Look again at paragraph 3 of Lia's review and at the evidence you gathered in the grid in Question 4. Write a paragraph analysing what Lia thought about the set design. Use these sentences to start:

> Lia loved the set design. In particular, she liked the…

Check your progress:

I understand what it means to analyse or review.

I can select evidence to analyse from another text.

I can select, analyse and use evidence in the form of quotations.

Checklist for success:

✔ Comment in particular on what she focused on in paragraph 3 about the set design.

✔ Use some of her *actual words or phrases* as evidence of her thoughts and opinions.

✔ Put her actual words in speech marks.

Analysing the presentation of plays

You will learn how to:
- follow the layout of a play
- compare different conventions of plays and stories.

There are many different ways to recount events or describe feelings or experiences. Two of the most common forms writers choose are plays and stories. These two forms look different when written down.

Introducing the skills

1 Think of a well-known fairy story, myth or legend. Consider all the different ways that story has been told:

   a) Is there a song about it, or a film?

   b) How was it *originally* told?

Read the two extracts below.

Text A

Both my father and I were extremely hungry, so we were delighted to see a tasty feast laid out for us. Perhaps the Beast was not as fearsome as he sounded, I wondered? Feeling less frightened we both sat down and began to eat.

Suddenly, I heard the deafening sound of footsteps approaching, and a voice roared, 'BEAUTY – I have come for you!'

'I won't leave you!' cried my father.

'You must,' I whispered, as the door slowly opened...

Text B

BEAUTY sits alone singing the ballad from Act 1.

She has made a coronet of flowers and is weaving them into her hair.

[...]

FATHER arrives and is just finishing a meal.

The song is interrupted by a huge roar of 'Beauty!'

Enter **BEAST'S MAN**.

BEAST'S MAN: It's time.

FATHER: No.

He wraps his arms around BEAUTY.

by Laurence Boswell

Vocabulary

Beast's man: the beast's servant

2 Write short answers to these questions:

a) Which well-known fairy-tale are both texts based on?

b) Do the same people appear in both stories?

c) Which one do you think comes from a **play script**, and which one from a storybook? What makes you think this?

Key term

play script: the words and actions from a play written down for the actors to use

3 Look at the list below of different features of presentation from Texts A and B. Identify the places in Texts A and B where you can see each one. For example:

'I won't leave you!' cried my father. ——— speech marks

a) There is a main character telling us what happens using the pronoun 'I'.

b) There are speech marks when someone speaks.

c) The writer tells us what a character is doing or how they are behaving.

d) The way people behave is written in the past tense.

e) The way people behave is in the present tense.

f) Uses full sentences.

g) Uses lines and sentences that are short, like notes.

h) All the names of the characters who speak are on the left-hand side of the page in a line going down.

i) Uses the words 'enter' or 'exit' to show when someone appears or leaves.

4 Now decide which of these features are from a play and which are from a story. Copy the grid below and put each feature in the correct column. Two have been done for you.

Play	Story
h)	b)

Developing the skills

Writers choose how to present a story for particular reasons. For example, if you are learning a part for a play, it is easy to find the words you have to say if your character's name is listed down the left-hand side of the page.

In the play, you have to work out what people are thinking. You can only do this by hearing what they say or looking at how they behave. Writers use **stage directions** to indicate how an actor should say their lines or show how they should move:

> FATHER: No.
>
> *He wraps his arms around BEAUTY.*

Key term

stage direction: information provided by the writer of a play which tells the actor what to do or how to speak

Stage directions, written in the present tense

5 What does the stage direction in the example above suggest about how Beauty's father feels? Choose one of these options.

a) He feels protective and is worried what will happen.

b) He is angry with her.

c) He is frightened and wants her help.

6 Which of the following examples from another part of the play is the *correct* way to set out a play script?

Version A	Version B	Version C
BEAUTY struggles to free herself from her FATHER.	BEAUTY struggled to free herself from her FATHER.	BEAUTY struggles to free herself from her FATHER.
BEAUTY: I must go, Father!	BEAUTY said, 'I must go, Father!'	BEAUTY: 'I must go, Father!'

7 What is *incorrect* about the other two versions?

    a) Version [A/B/C] is incorrect because…

    b) Version [A/B/C] is incorrect because…

Applying the skills

Read this extract from later in the story:

Beauty was desperate for news of her family, and wept and wept. Quietly, the Beast entered her room.

'What is it?' he asked, tenderly, his growl less severe than before.

'I…miss my family,' she said, sadly.

Beast held out a mirror. It sparkled in the light and seemed to change colour as Beauty took it from his rough hands.

'Here,' he said. 'Look into the mirror and it will tell you all you need to know.'

Slowly, he paced out of the room.

8 Turn this part of the story into a play script. Use the opening below, then continue in the same style:

> *BEAUTY sits on a bench looking out of the window.*
>
> BEAUTY (*weeping*): Where are you father? I miss you and the rest of the family so much!

9 When you have finished, write some brief notes explaining *what* you did (for example, 'put name of speaker on left'). You could write these on sticky notes and stick them on your play script.

Checklist for success:

- ✔ Write the names of characters on the left-hand side of the page in capitals.
- ✔ Write what people say without speech marks.
- ✔ Include stage and speech directions.
- ✔ Use the present tense for describing how people speak or move.

Check your progress:

I can identify the differences between the form of stories and plays.

I can comment on the differences between plays and stories, and identify examples.

I can change a prose version into a play version using the correct conventions.

Discussing key ideas from a text

You will learn how to:
- develop your skills as a speaker and listener in a group
- analyse carefully through discussing ideas.

What sort of speaker and listener are you when you are in a group? Do you generally keep quiet and let others do the talking? Do you shout things out or interrupt others? It is important to understand the skills you need to take part in group discussions.

Introducing the skills

Think about the main characters and events in the fairy-tale *Cinderella*. Discuss it in small groups – do you all agree on the plot?

Now read this text about *Cinderella*.

The most famous version of Cinderella is probably by the French author, Charles Perrault (1628–1703). In his version, Cinderella (named because she would curl up and sleep near the **cinders** of the fire to keep warm) is the daughter of a widowed king who has married again to a woman with two unpleasant daughters. When a handsome Prince invites everyone to a **ball**, she cries as she is unable to go, but a Fairy Godmother miraculously appears. She turns a pumpkin into a golden carriage, mice into horses, a rat into a coachman, and lizards into footmen. She also turns Cinderella's rags into a jewelled gown, and gives her a delicate pair of glass slippers. The Godmother warns Cinderella that she must return before midnight, as that is when the spells end.

After winning the Prince's heart and amazing everyone (who *is* the mysterious beauty?) she remembers to leave in time. But at the next ball, she loses track of time and suddenly has to run off, but in her haste, she leaves behind a glass slipper. Desperate to find who the girl is, the Prince orders his servants to find the owner of the slipper. When the servants arrive at Cinderella's house, the two sisters try to force the slipper on to their feet but of course it doesn't fit. Cinderella tries it on, and it does! She and the Prince live happily ever after.

Vocabulary

cinders: ashes

ball: a glamorous party with music and dancing

However, the earliest versions of the story go back almost 2000 years! An Italian writer, Giambattista Basile, had already come up with his own version in 1634, in which a girl called Zozella is mistreated by her six stepsisters. The fairy in Basile's story comes out of a magic tree that Zozella has planted, and although she dresses her in fine clothes, there are no pumpkin, mice or lizards. The idea of the slipper being left behind is the same, but it isn't a glass one.

In the Brothers Grimm version, poor Cinderella's clothing for the ball is provided by a white bird in a magic tree that grows from her mother's grave. There is also a Norwegian version called 'Katie Woodencloak', but in that tale, it isn't a ball she attends, but a church service. In some versions, the wicked stepmother or governess is a wicked step*father.* In another, the shoe is magical and changes size and shape so that it will only fit Cinderella.

It has been said that there are over 300 versions of the tale!

1 Scan the text, then write down your answers to the following questions using full sentences.

  a) Whose version is considered the most well-known?

  b) What seem to be the common elements in all versions?

  c) How many versions of the story are there, approximately?

2 Why do you think Cinderella has been such a popular story across the world, and for so long?

Open questions like Question 2 can be more difficult to answer. Discussing them with other people can help, but how can you make sure the discussion succeeds?

Here, four students discuss Question 2:

Jay: Well, it's obvious. Every girl wants to meet a handsome prince, don't they?

Sia: That's rubbish! You're just stupid...

Levi: My favourite Disney film is The Jungle Book.

Daz: Ok, Levi, but we're supposed to be talking about why...

Jay: (shouts before he can finish) No one wants to hear your opinion, Daz.

3 Which student:

   a) disagrees with Jay in an unpleasant way and does not give reasons?

   b) goes off the point and talks about something else?

   c) interrupts rudely?

4 Which speaker is the most polite and sensible?

5 How could the discussion be improved? Think about:

   a) what Sia could have said

   b) what Levi could have talked about

   c) how Jay could have supported Daz.

In a discussion it is vital that you:

- take turns to speak: listen carefully to what other people say, even if you disagree
- don't interrupt or make rude, personal comments
- encourage others to speak
- speak politely
- stick to the point of the discussion
- give reasons for your point of view.

6 Working in groups, answer Question 2 again. Try to make sure everyone gets a chance to speak. You can encourage them by saying things like:

> *What do you think?*

> *That's interesting. Tell us more...*

Applying the skills

7 Work in groups of three or four. Carry out the following task, sent to you by a famous film director, Simon Spielbug. Your group should discuss your ideas and agree your approach, ready to present to Simon.

Hi team! I want to make a brand new film of 'Cinderella' but it needs to be DIFFERENT from the famous one. Can you come up with some new ideas for me? You can change as much as you like but it must still be obvious to the audience that it is Cinderella. I want to know the main plot, who the characters are, and how it will be different.

Simon.

Check your progress:

I can give my opinion in a group discussion and keep to the set task.

I can give my opinion politely and offer reasons to support it.

I can give my opinions with reasons, listen to others and encourage everyone in the group during a discussion.

Checklist for success:

✔ Make sure your group is clear about the task and what the aim is.

✔ Follow the advice for effective group discussions.

Analysing a poem's shape, sound and structure

You will learn how to:

- analyse a poem's shape, sound and structure
- explore how a writer uses gothic ideas to make a poem memorable.

Poets set out their words on the page in a particular order to create the effect they want. They decide how long lines should be, how the poem should be divided up (if at all), and whether it needs any special sound patterns.

Introducing the skills

> **1** Look at the picture.
>
> **a)** Where do you think this door is?
>
> **b)** Who – or what – might be behind it?
>
> **c)** If the door was from a story, what sort of story might it be?

Read this text from a book about types or genres of stories.

The gothic

Towards the end of the eighteenth century in Britain and in Europe, writers started to tell stories, compose plays and create poems that people called 'gothic'. The main characters were often young people (for example, girls or orphans) in terrible danger from cruel older men or women. The plots were full of mystery and suspense; often readers did not know what was going to happen to the hero or heroine until the very end of the tale. Some stories involved one character seeking revenge on another, or turning from being good to evil. They often contained supernatural happenings, murders or disappearances. The settings were often scary, dark castles, crumbling ruins or mansions, found in mountainous landscapes or wild forests. Typical titles were: *The Mysteries of Udolpho*, *The Castle of Otranto* and, famously, *Dracula*.

2 What have you learned about gothic literature from this text? Answer these questions with one sentence each:

 a) What sorts of plot did gothic stories have?

 b) What sorts of people were in them?

 c) What were typical settings for these stories?

 d) What well-known gothic stories are mentioned?

3 Write a list of any other stories you know that could be called 'gothic', or which have elements of the gothic in them.

Read this poem. As you read, think about what happens in the poem – is it 'gothic'? If so, in what ways?

In a Far Land

In a far land
a black mountain broods:
beneath the black mountain
stretch the green woods.

Among the green woods
a white castle soars:
in the white castle
are dark corridors.

The corridors lead
to a black, shut door.
Behind it a Prince
sprawls dead on the floor.

With a cobwebbed cup
by his withered hand,
a Prince lies poisoned
in that far land.

A hobbling old Princess
creeps to that door –
ghost calling ghost
for evermore!

She murmurs her guilt
In sighs and soft moans.
Behind the locked door
the dead Prince groans.

by Raymond Wilson

4 To understand how the poem works, answer these questions about its *structure*:

   a) What does the poet describe in the first two **verses**?

   b) How is the last line of the first verse linked to the first line of the second verse?

   c) What other patterns like this can you see in the first two verses?

Key term

verse: a section of a poem divided into lines, often with rhyming words at the end of some lines

5 Why do you think the poet chose to tell the story in this way? In pairs, discuss each of these possibilities:

   a) He wanted the reader to be like someone following a camera as it zooms in from a long way away.

   b) He wanted the reader to be surprised by the final line.

   c) He wanted to help the reader learn new words by repeating them more than once.

Developing the skills

The poem 'In a Far Land' is a bit like a ballad – a rhyming poem that tells a story, which was often spoken aloud before it was written down.

6 Write down the pairs of rhymes from each verse. Do they match exactly?

7 Learn one verse from the poem, then speak it aloud. How easy was it?

8 Why do you think ballads (story poems) used rhymes? Discuss this in pairs.

9 The poet also uses sounds in another way. Which four words from the final verse sound like the noise they are describing? (Hint: the first one is 'murmurs'.)

By analysing the shape, sound and structure of the poem, you can see how the reader is led on a mysterious journey to find out what is behind the door. The poet has also used structure to surprise the reader and make them think.

10 Look at the last two verses.

a) What words, phrases or lines give you information that does not seem to make sense?

b) What questions would you ask the princess or prince if you could speak to them?

11 In your pairs, talk about what *you* think has happened.

Applying the skills

12 Write three paragraphs about the way Raymond Wilson presents and structures his poem and why you think it is effective:

a) In the first paragraph, write about how each verse develops the story.

b) In the second paragraph, comment on sounds and patterns.

c) In the third paragraph, write about how Wilson makes the reader think and ask questions.

Checklist for success:

✔ Focus on structure – for example, the order of verses.

✔ Think about why Wilson has ordered things in the way he has.

✔ Comment on what is particularly effective about the last two verses.

Check your progress:

I can identify verses and basic rhymes in a poem.

I can comment on the use of patterns, verses and sounds in poems.

I can comment on the effect of a poet's choices in terms of structures and sounds.

Introducing key points when analysing texts

You will learn how to:
- make a clear point about a detail in a text
- use linking words or phrases when talking or writing about two texts.

When analysing a text, it is important to support your ideas by using relevant quotations from the text.

Introducing the skills

Read this paragraph, in which a student is writing about the structure of the poem 'In a Far Land' from Topic 6.4.

> In the first verse, the poet presents a picture of a mysterious landscape. The second line mentions a 'black mountain' which creates a gloomy mood.

Explains the *part of the poem overall* that is being analysed.

Explains where *in the verse itself* a word or phrase is being selected.

Gives the *chosen phrase* (not the whole line).

1 Which quotation has the student selected?

2 What effect does the student say these words have?

3 Which one of these verbs could the student also have quoted to show the gloomy mood?

a) 'broods'

b) 'soars'

c) 'lead'.

Developing the skills

Words or phrases that indicate place or position in the text can help to make your analysis really precise.

Read another paragraph from the student's analysis.

> The second verse links back to the first verse. We can see this in the first line, where the poet repeats 'the green woods'. This makes it sound like a child's memory game and fits the fairy-tale style.

4 Which word tells us the verse to look at?

5 Which word tells us which line to look at?

6 Which quotation has the student selected for comment?

In the example above, the student began with the **demonstrative** 'This', which refers back to the most recent point. The writer does not have to tell the reader again what the focus is.

Here are some words and phrases that can help you be precise in your analysis:

Words/phrases showing the order of things	Words/phrases that help make links
firstly, initially, to start with	in the same way, similarly, as well as, also, both [verses show…]
next, then, later, afterwards, after that	
finally, at the end, at the conclusion, in the last verse	in contrast, however, yet, but

The words and phrases in the right-hand column are useful for showing how two things are alike or different.

7 Choose a suitable word or phrase from the grid to make this analysis clear:

> In the third verse of the poem, we are told the prince 'sprawls dead on the floor'. …
> in the final line, he seems to be alive as he 'groans'.

Applying the skills

8 Copy and complete this paragraph of analysis. Use words and phrases from the grid above to help you:

> …the writer tells us the old princess is actually a spirit as the line says, 'ghost calling ghost'. …, in the…verse, we learn that the prince is a phantom as the final line says, 'the dead prince groans'.

Check your progress:

I can use some linking words and phrases when analysing texts.

I can use linking words to help me be precise in how I analyse in a text.

I can select quotations carefully and use linking words for precise analysis.

Comparing two poems using analysis skills

You will learn how to:

- analyse the shape and structure of two poems on a similar theme
- comment on modern and traditional approaches to fairy-tales.

Your task

Write three or four paragraphs comparing two poems on the same theme, commenting on:

- the story they tell
- their shape and structure.

Think about the fairy-story *Jack and the Beanstalk*. A boy sells the family cow to a man he meets for some magic seeds. His mother is very angry and throws the seeds away, but in the morning a huge beanstalk has grown. Jack climbs up the beanstalk and there he finds a magic land. He has to hide from a man-eating giant who has many precious belongings, including a magic harp. Can you remember – or guess – what happened to Jack in the rest of the story?

Read the two poems below.

The Magic Seeds

There was an old woman who sowed a corn seed,
And from it there sprouted a tall yellow weed.
She planted the seeds of the tall yellow flower,
And up sprang a blue one in less than an hour.
The seed of the blue one she sowed in a bed,
And up sprang a tall tree with blossoms of red.
And high in the treetop there sang a white bird,
And his song was the sweetest that ever was heard.
The people they came from far and from near,
The song of the little white bird for to hear.

by James Reeves

(This is the second part of a poem based on the fairy-tale.)

Jack and the Beanstalk, Part 2

But overnight the tiny seeds grew and grew and grew and grew into a

      H U G E

                  B the top

    reached   E

                  A till he

       up   N

                  S quickly

                  T

    climbed   A

                  L   Jack

                  K which

by Mike Gould

Approaching the task

Before you write your comparison, copy and complete the grid below to help you plan your ideas.

Feature	'The Magic Seeds'	'Jack and the Beanstalk, Part 2'
story (what we are told happens in the poem)		
structure and layout (how the poem is set out on the page)		
language choices (use of particular words, phrases, sounds, rhymes, etc.)		
anything else		

1 Using your comparison grid, now draft your paragraphs.

   a) Begin with two paragraphs – one on each poem.

   b) Then add at least one more paragraph, comparing and contrasting them.

Checklist for success:

- ✔ Select particular words, phrases, lines or patterns and say something clear about what they show the reader.
- ✔ Use connectives to show links or differences between the poems.
- ✔ Use precise words to show what part of the poem you are referring to.
- ✔ Use speech marks to indicate words or phrases that come from the poem.

Reflecting on your progress

Response 1

1 The poet tells a story about a flower that grows from seeds. It has one verse and that shows how the seed **2** grows and changes from one thing to another so that **3** by the end there is a tree with a bird that sings. It sounds like a fairy-tale because there is magic which makes the flowers change colour. 'The seed of the blue one' at first **4** then 'blossoms of red.'

1 Makes a clear point about the 'story' of the poem.

2 Comments on the structure, but does not explain why or what effect it has.

3 Comments on what occurs at the end of the poem.

4 Gives quotations in speech marks.

Comment on Response 1

This is a fair start at analysing the structure of the first poem, but it is not very precise. The student needs to refer to where lines occur, give more information about them and explain how this helps the story.

2 Using the comments above and progress points 1b–5b in the Check your progress section at the end of this chapter, rewrite this response to improve it.

Response 2

1 The poet describes how an 'old woman' plants magic seeds that eventually produce a tree with a bird that sings beautifully. This is a typical fairy-tale situation. The poem **2** sounds like a rhyme you are meant to remember because each line comes from the one before, and tells about a bigger thing that grows. For example, the first two lines **3** of the poem are about the single 'corn seed' that becomes a 'yellow weed'.

1 Gives a good summary sentence of the whole poem's 'story'.

2 Makes a comment but does not really explain it.

3 A well-chosen quotation gives evidence about how the structure works.

Comment on Response 2

This response focuses clearly on the story and the structure of the first poem, and is precise about which words and phrases are selected and where they occur. The student has commented on how this is like a typical fairy-tale, but has not really explained in what way or been precise about what aspects fit this genre.

3 Using the comments above and progress points 1c–5c in the Check your progress section at the end of this chapter, rewrite this response to improve it.

Check your progress

1a	I can focus on particular elements of a text.
2a	I can follow the layout of a play.
3a	I can offer some opinions in a group discussion.
4a	I can identify verses and simple rhymes in a poem.
5a	I can identify linking words and phrases in a text.
1b	I can choose evidence to help me analyse a text.
2b	I can follow the layout of a play and identify how it differs from a story.
3b	I can state my opinion on a set task politely during a discussion, giving reasons to support it.
4b	I can identify shapes, sounds and structures in a poem.
5b	I can identify the main points in a text and give a personal response to it.
1c	I can analyse a text using relevant quotations as evidence.
2c	I can identify and use the different conventions of plays and stories.
3c	I can analyse through group discussion, giving my opinions and encouraging others to give theirs.
4c	I can analyse a poem's shape, sound and structure and explain how ideas are used to make it memorable.
5c	I can choose a range of quotations and linking words for precise analysis or comparison.

Chapter 7
Testing your skills

What's it all about?

In this chapter you will have a chance to practise some of the skills that you have been introduced to in the book by answering some exam-style questions. This will enable you to assess the strengths and weaknesses of your answers by looking at sample answers and comments from teachers, before you move on to the next stage of the course.

You will learn how to:
- apply your learning independently
- answer exam-style questions
- work under timed conditions.

You will:
- answer the questions on two examination-style papers.
- mark your work using examination-style mark schemes
- consider how you could improve your answers in the future.

Reading and writing questions on non-fiction texts

Task 1: Reading

Read the extract from an information text that explores and suggests answers to well-known mysteries – in this case, what are mermaids?

The Sirenia (Sea Cow) Theory

It seems there is no evidence for a mermaid-like 'missing link' between fish and humans. So, many scientists have turned instead to creatures already known to exist. Is it possible that one of these animals
5 is sometimes mistaken for mermaid?

The sea cow

At first, sea cows may seem like an unlikely candidate. Instead of slender, graceful figures, sea cows have large, cucumber-shaped bodies and weigh over eight times as much as the average human. At 4 metres (13 feet), they
10 are also over twice as long. Their skin is rough and grey, and instead of arms, they have rounded flippers.

But some scientists are so sure sea cows are the 'mermaids' that have been reported that they have named this group of mammals 'sirenians' after the sea-dwelling creatures known as sirens in ancient Greek myths. Sirenians include all three species of manatees
15 and the dugong.

Sea cows and mermaids: separated at birth?

Mermaids and sea cows (manatees or dugongs) do share some surprising similarities. As mammals, sea cows must occasionally rise to the surface to breathe air – and they do so head first, just like humans. Female manatees and dugongs have breasts and could resemble a woman, especially when they rise out of the water to suckle their young.
20 Their short, paddle-like flippers allow sea cows to swim gracefully – and could even be mistaken for short human arms. Since sea cows feed on sea grass in shallow waters, they are also likely to be spotted by observers near the shore.

From *Mermaids (Solving Mysteries with Science)* by Lori Hile

Now answer the following questions.

1 Which word in paragraph 1 suggests that people who think that sea cows are mermaids are wrong? (1)

2 Explain in your own words the meaning of the word 'unlikely' as it is used in paragraph 2. (1)

3 Which of these statements is a fact about sea cows? (1)

   a) Sea cows are slender and graceful.

   b) Sea cows weigh more than humans.

   c) Sea cows have arms.

   d) Sea cows have grey scales.

4 Which word in paragraph 2 suggests that sea cows are big? (1)

5 What does using the word 'But' at the start of paragraph 3 suggest? (1)

6 Which word in paragraph 3 has a suffix? (1)

7 Write a suitable sub-heading for paragraph 3. (2)

8 Find an adjective in paragraph 4 which shows that the writer did not expect manatees and mermaids to be alike. (1)

9 Write three ways in which sea cows are like humans. (2)

10 Explain in your own words the meaning of each of the following, as it is used in the text. (2)

   a) dwelling (line 13)

   b) spotted (line 22).

Total (13)

Read this extract from later in the same information text.

Cryptozoology and Other Hypotheses

Three-quarters of all mermaid sightings occur in waters where no seals or sea cows live. How can we explain these sightings? Cryptozoologists propose that mermaids are creatures that have not yet been
5   discovered.

Cryptozoology

Cryptozoology is the search for animals whose existence has not been proven, such as Bigfoot, unicorns or mermaids. To strengthen their case, cryptozoologists point to the recent discovery of the Megamouth shark.
10   This 750-kilogram (1,653-pound), 4.5 metre- (15-foot-) long fish was completely unknown until members of the US Navy pulled it from the bottom of the sea in 1976. Its discovery makes us wonder: What other undiscovered creatures could lurk in our waters?

But is cryptozoology a 'real' science?

15   Most scientists do not recognise cryptozoology as an official branch of science. Although scientists agree that thousands of unknown animals exist – particularly insects – they criticise cryptozoologists for focusing their efforts mostly on exciting and
20   elusive (hard to find) creatures, like mermaids, despite little scientific support for their existence. But cryptozoologists point out that many real animals including giant pandas were once believed to only exist in myths.

From *Mermaids (Solving Mysteries with Science)* by Lori Hile

Now answer the following questions.

11   What is the main purpose of this text? (1)

12   Write down the statement that most accurately reflects what cryptozoologists think mermaids are. (1)

   a)   Mermaids aren't seals or sea cows.

   b)   Mermaids aren't real.

   c)   Mermaids are a new type of animal.

13 Write down a phrase from paragraph 2 which shows that the writer is giving examples to make her meaning clearer. (1)

14 What is the underlined word an example of? (1)
Its discovery makes <u>us</u> wonder.

15 Write a summary of 70–90 words explaining why cryptozoology could provide the answer to the mystery of what a mermaid is. (5)

16 Why does the writer use a pair of dashes in paragraph 3? (1)

17 Divide the following complex sentence into a series of shorter ones, using any punctuation that you consider appropriate. You may change wording slightly to retain agreement and clarity. (2)

> Although scientists agree that thousands of unknown animals exist – particularly insects – they criticise cryptozoologists for focusing their efforts mostly on exciting and elusive (hard to find) creatures, like mermaids, despite little scientific support for their existence.

Total (12)

Task 2: Writing

Write a news article for a local paper about the sighting of a possible mermaid or other creature of legend such as a unicorn or dragon.

You will need to:

- choose a creature or invent a new one
- use the language and structure of a news article to help make the information clear – for example, headline, standfirst…

Do not include illustrations or any other layout features.

Write your plan out first.

Total (25)

Reading and writing questions on fiction texts

Task 3: Reading

Read this passage from *Ingo* by Helen Dunmore, about a girl called Sapphire and her adventures under the sea when she meets Faro, who is half boy, half seal.

'Look around, Sapphire, and tell me what else you've *noticed*,' he challenges.

I peer through the water:

'Well, rocks – over there, look sharp ones.
5   I wouldn't want to go near them. And there's a fish! Just going out of sight, look, it's a really big one.'

'Huge,' Faro agrees. 'It must be at least as big as this,' and he puts his hands a few centimetres apart. 'What else have you noticed?'

10   'Um – is that a **current** over there? And I think I saw something scuttling down on the sea bed just now – but it's so far down, it's hard to tell—'

'Anything else?'

'I noticed that shark, anyway. And you didn't.'

15   'All right. My turn.' A rush of sound pours out of Faro's mouth.

'Faro, I can't understand—'

'I know you can't. I'm not talking to you.
I'm asking everyone who is here to come out where
20   you can see them.'

The sea around us begins to thicken. Two grey seals slide by, twisting as they go. They turn and circle, almost touching us. They have big eyes like retriever dogs, and they look as if they're laughing. Their nostrils
25   are closed tight and their whiskers are flattened against

Vocabulary

current: area of water moving in a specific direction

muzzle: part of the face between nose and chin

mercury: a silvery grey coloured chemical element

their **muzzles**. But how strong they are, how powerful. Their muscles ripple under their skin as they go by. A dazzling cloud of silver fish flickers in and out between my fingers like droplets of **mercury**.

30 I look to my left and there's a huge flatfish, as big as our kitchen table, with one popeye goggling at me. One after another a raft of purple jellyfish floats past, tentacles drifting, their jelly skirts bellying in and out, in and out…

35 'So that's how they move,' I whisper. Their tentacles are thick and snaky and have suckers all the way down – what if one of them whipped across my leg? They look as if they would sting. I scull backwards, out of range. The jellyfish sail on in a line, like battleships now,
40 making for war.

'Look down there,' says Faro, and a giant spider crab appears out of a whirl of sand, and then another. Conor hates spider crabs. I can always frighten him by picking up a dead one on the shore and chasing after him with
45 it, flapping its claws. But I wouldn't touch one of these.

The sand settles and shows an angler fish, almost buried but for the shine of her lure. Dad caught one once when he was deep-sea fishing, and showed it to me. 'It lives far out, on the sea bottom. They're adapted
50 to the dark. Just as well, poor creature, it's ugly as sin. It wouldn't want to see itself in the light.'

'Look up,' says Faro, and I see a soup of plankton shimmering in the light from the surface. And right above us there's another shark, much smaller but the
55 same shape as the other little-feeder. A shoal of tiny grey fish darts to the side, away from the sieving jaws. And that rock there – it's covered with dog whelks, thickly striped. More fish flick past – and here's a herd of sea horses riding the curve of Faro's tail—

60 'It's not fair. You made them come. All these creatures weren't here when I was looking.'

From *Ingo* by Helen Dunmore

Now answer the following questions.

1 Which of the statements below best sums up this extract? (1)

a) It is about a girl who is scared of what she sees in the water.

b) It is about a girl who begins to see what has been around her in the water all the time.

c) It is about a girl who learns to live under water.

2 Whose viewpoint is this story told from? (1)

3 Re-read the paragraph that begins 'The sea around us began...'. In your own words, describe the way the writer has used sentence lengths and structures to describe the seals. (5)

4 The writer uses a dash once in line 17 when Sapphire is speaking to Faro. Why does the writer use this dash? (1)

5 Which word used in paragraph 11 suggests that the fish are brightly coloured? (1)

6 Read this sentence from the passage:

I look to my left and there's a huge flatfish, as big as our kitchen table, with one popeye goggling at me.

What two things are compared in this sentence? (1)

7 Find two examples of imagery used to describe the jellyfish. (2)

8 What do the words 'I scull backwards' suggest about Sapphire's feelings towards the jellyfish? (2)

9 Why does the writer use an ellipsis at the end of the paragraph describing the jellyfish? (1)

10 Which word in line 42 tells you that the spider crabs move quickly? (1)

11 Re-read lines 1–20. Describe the relationship between Faro and Sapphire as shown in this extract. (4)

12 How is Sapphire feeling during this extract? (5)

Total (25)

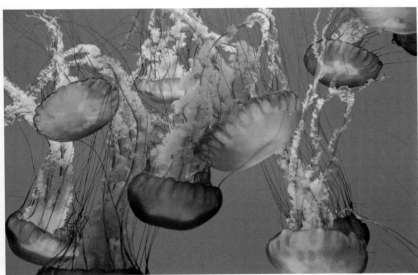

Task 4: Writing

In the passage you have read, Sapphire discovers a whole new world where she does not expect it.

Write a description of your own about a place where things change or are revealed that you did not expect.

You will need to consider:

- **setting:** where are you going to be for your description?
- **character:** are there any other characters?
- **plot:** why do things happen in this way? What do you do/feel?

Total (25)

Assess your progress: non-fiction reading and writing

In this section of the chapter you are going to look at your answers and some suggestions about what you could have written. You can then use these to see how you can improve your answers and assess your strengths and weaknesses.

Task 1: Reading questions on non-fiction texts

1 Which word in paragraph 1 suggests that people who think that sea cows are mermaids are wrong?

Answer: 'mistaken' (1)

Where might you have gone wrong?

It seems that there is no evidence for a mermaid-like 'missing link' between fish and humans. So, many scientists have turned instead to creatures already known to exist. Is it possible that one of these animals is sometime mistaken for a mermaid?

Some students would see 'no evidence' and think that this is the answer, but actually this phrase is about earlier theories of what mermaids could be.

Always check the rest of the sentence or short paragraph before you decide on your answer.

2 Explain in your own words the meaning of the word 'unlikely' as it is used in the text in paragraph two. (1)

Answer: not much evidence for this idea/not a good fit and therefore slow to come to mind

Where might you have gone wrong?

You might have misread the text and thought the word was 'likely' or you may have thought it was about whether or not something was going to happen.

You need to read the whole sentence as the word is used to describe whether or not sea cows are a probable candidate for a mismatch.

3 Which of these statements is a fact about sea cows?

a) Sea cows are slender and graceful.

b) Sea cows weigh more than humans.

c) Sea cows have arms.

d) Sea cows have grey scales.

Answer: b) *Sea cows weigh more than humans (1)*

Where might you have gone wrong?

If you picked answer a) then you may have scanned for the key words from the question and when you found them, looked no further. Actually the passage says 'instead of slender, graceful figures', which means that they *do not* have this appearance. Always read the whole sentence.

Answer b) is correct as the passage tells us that they weigh eight times more than us. You might have missed this if you were looking for the word 'more', but in this case you could infer the correct answer.

If you answered c) then you were misled by finding the word 'arms' in the passage, but actually it said 'instead of arms'. Remember to read *around* the key word.

If you picked answer d) then you did not read carefully enough. Sea cows have grey *skin* not scales.

4 Which word in paragraph 2 suggests that sea cows are big?

Answer: large (1)

Where might you have gone wrong?

The paragraph contains several phrases that describe the sea cows as being long and heavy, but this is the only single word that suggests overall size. Look for the word that most precisely matches the meaning you are looking for. You may also have selected a phrase – be careful to only give one word if asked for it.

5 What does using the word 'But' at the start of paragraph 3 suggest?

Answer: that the scientists who believe that sea cows are mermaids do so <u>even though/despite the fact that</u> there is evidence to the contrary. (1 mark for any reasonable explanation)

Where might you have gone wrong?

You might have just said that 'But' is a conjunction. However, the question asks 'what', so you need to explain what the writer conveys with the word.

6 Which word in paragraph 3 has a suffix?

Answer: sirenians (1)

Where might you have gone wrong?

You may have copied out just the suffix – 'ians' – or explained the meaning of the word that contains the suffix. The question asks you to identify the word with the suffix, so you need to simply write out the full word.

7 Write a suitable sub-heading for paragraph 3.

Answer: A new name for sea cows/Scientists rename sea cows (or any similar answer that features scientists or reclassification). (1) mark for idea of new animal/classification plus (1) for mention of scientists/ experts.

Where might you have gone wrong?

You might have thought that sirenians were a new breed of animal and written something about this discovery. Or you may have read that a siren is a creature from Ancient Greek mythology and written about that. This type of question is testing whether or not you can pick out the main idea of a paragraph – these are just two pieces of information that contribute to the main idea, which is that some scientists are so certain that mermaids are sea cows that they have renamed sea cows to suggest this. If you struggle to identify the main idea, ask yourself what message the writer is trying to communicate.

8 Find an adjective in paragraph 4 which shows that the writer did not expect manatees and mermaids to be alike.

Answer: surprising (1)

Where might you have gone wrong?

You may have written out a phrase – for example, 'surprising similarities'. Unfortunately, you will not get any marks for this, as it is important to show that you know *exactly* which word is the correct answer.

9 Write three ways in which sea cows are like humans.

Answer:
They come out of the water head first.
They have breasts.
Their flippers could look like arms.
(3 correct = 2 marks; 1 or 2 correct = 1 mark)

Where might you have gone wrong?

You may not have identified all three similarities.

10 Explain in your own words the meaning of each of the following, as it is used in the text. (2)

a) dwelling

b) spotted.

Answer: a) living in/resident of, b) to be seen (briefly)

Where might you have gone wrong?

You may have been unsure of these words and so missed out the question. It is important to read the whole sentence and see if you can work out a meaning from the context.

11 What is the main purpose of this text? (1)

Answer: to explain to us (about cryptozoology and whether or not it is able to explain mermaids)

Where might you have gone wrong?

You may have stated what type of text this is, e.g. non-fiction, or what form – an information text.

12 Write down the statement that most accurately reflects what cryptozoologists think mermaids are.

a) Mermaids aren't seals or sea cows.

b) Mermaids aren't real.

c) Mermaids are a new type of animal.

Answer: c) Mermaids are a new type of animal. (1)

Where might you have gone wrong?

The text uses quite a few words which could suggest that cryptozoologists believe mermaids are a real thing: 'existence has not been proven', 'unknown', 'undiscovered'. If you did not read closely, you may have thought that they were saying that a mermaid was a Bigfoot or unicorn or a shark.

13 Write down a phrase from paragraph 2 which shows that the writer is giving examples to make her meaning clearer.

Answer: such as (1)

Where might you have gone wrong?

You might have skim read the question and thought you needed to find the examples: Bigfoot, unicorns or mermaids.

14 What is the underlined word an example of? Its discovery makes <u>us</u> wonder: (1)

Answer: inclusive language/pronouns/including the reader

Where might you have gone wrong?

You may not have remembered how writers use words such as this to make a connection with the reader. Always think carefully about the effect a word has on you if asked to comment on it specifically.

 15 Write a summary of 70–90 words explaining why cryptozoology could provide the answer to the mystery of what a mermaid is. (5)

Answer: 1 mark for each of the following

Mark	Answer	Further information
1	Identification of four main points.	Other theories don't explain all sightings. New things are being discovered all the time. Scientists agree that there are lots of unknown creatures. Some very real animals used to be considered to be fantastical.
1	Use of own words and not copying text too much.	
1	Organisation of ideas (the order and groupings of ideas that you include).	
1	Accuracy of language. Your choice of grammar, spelling and punctuation.	
1	Word length of 70–90 words.	

7 .3

Where might you have gone wrong?

You may not have found all the points. Remember that the number of marks shown is a clue to the number of points needed in your answer. You may have given lots of examples rather than sticking to the point. You might not have realised that some of the information given could support cryptozoology if you had not considered the inferences you could draw from the text.

16 Why does the writer use a pair of dashes in paragraph 3?

Answer: to separate out an additional piece of information. (1)

Where might you have gone wrong?

You may not have thought that dashes were used in this way, as commas are used in this way in formal texts. However, this text is quite informal and so the dashes are appropriate.

17 Divide the following complex sentence into two shorter ones, using any punctuation that you consider appropriate. You may change wording slightly to retain agreement and clarity.

> Although scientists agree that thousands of unknown animals exist – particularly insects – they criticise cryptozoologists for focusing their efforts mostly on exciting and elusive (hard to find) creatures, like mermaids, despite little scientific support for their existence.

Answer: 1 mark for each correct sentence. You will need to check that each sentence begins with a capital letter and ends with a full stop. You should check that each one makes sense on its own and contains a subject, object and verb.

Where might you have gone wrong?

You might have struggled to make this into shorter sentences and keep the meaning the same. Remember that the question allows you to alter the wording a little.

Task 2: Writing

Use the table below to self-assess your answer to these questions. You may find it helpful to highlight using a different colour when you find evidence of what you have done well. Remember that your teacher will also look at your spelling, punctuation and sentence structures before you can award yourself a level.

Purpose and audience	Text structure
It is sometimes clear who you are writing for and you have used a few of the features of a news article. You have sometimes written as a journalist in your article.	You have tried to write your ideas in the order of a news article but end up telling a story or including elements of a TV interview.
It is often clear who you are writing for and you have used many of the features of a news article. You have almost always written as a journalist in your article.	Your article often follows the usual structure of a news article with a headline, sub-heading, introductory paragraph and then a re-telling in more detail with quotations from sources.
It is clear who you are writing for and you have used the features of a news article. You have written as a journalist all through your article.	Your article follows the usual structure of a news article with a headline, sub-heading, introductory paragraph and then a re-telling in more detail with quotations from sources.

Assess your progress: fiction reading and writing

Task 3: Reading questions on a fiction text

1 Which of the statements below best sums up this extract?

a) It is about a girl who is scared of what she sees in the water.

b) It is about a girl who begins to see what has been around her in the water all the time.

c) It is about a girl who learns to live under water.

Answer: b) It is about a girl who begins to see what has been around her in the water all the time. (1)

Where might you have gone wrong?

This question is about selecting the main point of the extract. It is true that at times Sapphire seems scared. She definitely learns to swim under water at the start of the extract. However, the main idea that recurs throughout the extract is that she sees the underwater world clearly and fully for the first time.

2 Whose viewpoint is this story told from? (1)

Answer: Sapphire's

Where might you have gone wrong?

You may have read the opening and scanned the rest and noticed that Faro speaks a lot during this extract. This may have led you to assume it is from his viewpoint. You need to read the whole text carefully, paying particular attention to pronouns.

3 Re-read the paragraph that begins 'The sea around us began...' In your own words, describe the way the writer has used sentence lengths and structures to describe the seals.

Answer: 1 mark each for the following comments:
Seals' movement is described in shorter sentences than their appearance. (1)
Most sentences are similar in structure with a main and subordinate clause. (1)
Most sentences start with they or their. (1)
Add 1 mark for each comment about the effect of these structures. For example, reflects the movement of the seals 'twisting'; suggests she is staring/cannot take her eyes off them.

Where might you have gone wrong?

You may have commented on the wrong sentences – always read the question carefully.

You may have counted the sentences or copied them out. The question asks you to describe the way that they are used, which means that you need to identify the types of sentences and structures using their names or other terminology that you have been taught.

You may not have scored all 5 marks. Remember to check how many marks are available, as this indicates how many comments you need to make.

4 The writer uses a dash once in line 17, when Sapphire is speaking to Faro. Why does the writer use this dash?

Answer: to show that he answers very quickly, interrupting her. (1)

Where might you have gone wrong?

You may have said that a dash is used to add information, but this is usually done with a pair of dashes around the information.

5 Which word used in paragraph 11 suggests that the fish are brightly coloured?

Answer: 'dazzling' (1)

Assess your progress: fiction reading and writing **191**

Where might you have gone wrong?

You may have written silver or mercury – however, these are not always bright in colour. The word 'dazzles' means that something blinds us with its glare so it is a word directly relating to brightness.

6 Read this sentence from the passage:

> I look to my left and there's a huge flatfish, as big as our kitchen table, with one popeye goggling at me.

What two things are compared in this sentence?

Answer: the flatfish and the kitchen table (1)

Where might you have gone wrong?

You may have copied out the whole sentence or added the extra details in which case you would not get any marks. Remember if you are asked for two things then you should only write two things.

7 Find two examples of imagery used to describe the jellyfish.

Answer: 1 mark for each of the following possible examples, to a maximum of 2 marks:
a raft of... (jellyfish) (1)
...purple (jellyfish) (1)
(jelly skirts) bellying in and out (1)
(NB: the words in the brackets are not necessary for the mark, but if you write them you will still get a mark.)

Where might you have gone wrong?

You may have copied out a full sentence that actually includes more than one example of imagery, but you would only receive 1 mark for this.

8 What do the words 'I scull backwards' suggest about Sapphire's feelings towards the jellyfish?

Answer: They suggest that she is scared/nervous/ apprehensive/feels in danger. (1)
Add 1 mark for a reasonable explanation – for example, as she moves away/out of harm's reach. (1)

Where might you have gone wrong?

You may have been uncertain what 'scull' means and so not tried to give an answer. Actually it is enough to know that she moved away from the jellyfish. Remember that understanding the gist of the text is often enough to attempt to answer a question.

9 Why does the writer use an ellipsis at the end of the paragraph describing the jellyfish?

Answer: To suggest time passing/that there were a lot of jellyfish/that they did not stop moving. 1 mark for any reasonable answer.

Where might you have gone wrong?

You may not have known what 'ellipsis' means and so given up, but the question also told you where it was, so it would have been possible to work it out.

10 Which word in line 42 tells you that the spider crabs move quickly? (1)

Answer: 'whirl' (1)

11 Re-read lines 1–20. Describe the relationship between Faro and Sapphire as shown in this extract. (4)

He is in control/ He is challenging/ bossy towards her	*Uses orders. The word 'challenge' is used.*
He is sarcastic	*He mocks her for thinking the fish is big. 'Huge,' Faro agrees. 'It must be at least as big as this,' and he puts his hands a few centimetres apart.*
She feels that he isn't fair to her	*'Faro, I can't understand—'*
She tries to regain some authority	*'I noticed that shark, anyway. And you didn't.'*

Answer: *Award 4 marks for two points with some development such as a quotation or reasoning for their ideas of each. 3 marks for two points with development of one. 2 points for two ideas or one idea and development.*

Where might you have gone wrong?

If you copied out extra words, such as 'of sand', then you would not get any marks because you would not have shown that you know precisely which word creates the effect.

12 How is Sapphire feeling during this extract?

Answer: *1 mark for each of the following points (up to 5) plus 1 mark each for a relevant quotation to go with the point.*

Point	Quote
uncertain	*'peer' 'Um – is that a current...'*
defensive	*'I noticed that shark...'*
confused	*'Faro, I can't understand –'*
awed	*''So that's how they move,' I whisper.'*
nervous	*'I scull backwards,'*
indignant/annoyed	*'It's not fair.'*

Where might you have gone wrong?

You may not have found all of the points or given quotations for them. Remember that the number of marks available is a clue to the amount you should write. You may also not have given quotations. Remember that if a question asks you to *explain*, it is looking for reasons to back up your ideas.

Task 4: Writing

Use the table below to self-assess your answer to these questions. You may find it helpful to highlight using a different colour when you find evidence of what you have done well. Remember that your teacher will also look at your spelling, punctuation and sentence structures before you can award yourself a level.

Purpose and audience	Text structure
It is clear that you are writing a description and you have created atmosphere and a sense of setting throughout your writing.	Your description is structured to lead the readers' eye or to encourage their senses rather than to develop a series of events or characterisation.
It is often clear that you are writing a description but sometimes you focus too much on telling a story or creating a character.	Your writing has episodes of imagery and atmosphere but may follow a narrative structure.
There are some pieces of description but your writing is mainly a story.	Your writing follows a narrative structure and the emphasis is on time passing and events.

Glossary of key terms

adjective: describes a noun (a thing), eg: the *chocolate* ice-cream

adverb: describes a verb (usually, an action), e.g. The dog growled *angrily*.

analyse: to study the essential features of a text in detail

anecdote: a short personal account of an interesting or humorous incident

argument texts: texts which consider both sides of the argument, but often end by favouring one side, e.g. feature articles, essays

atmosphere: the main mood or emotion in a piece of writing

audience: the group of people a text is written for

autobiography: the story of someone's life, written by themselves

biography: the story of someone's life, written by someone else

character: (in literature) a person in a story or play

clause: a group of words that includes a verb

connective: a linking word used in sentences. The standard ` words are: **and** – to add ideas together; **but** – to show contrast between ideas; **or** – to give an alternative; **so** – to lead from one idea to the next; **because** – to give a reason

connective phrase: a group of words used to link sentences or clauses such as 'Even though' or 'In the same way'

complex sentence: contains a supporting idea (subordinate clause), which adds to the information in the main idea (main clause)

compare: explain similarities or links between things

compound sentences: use connectives to join together equally-weighted simple sentences. You use compound sentences to build detail in writing, e.g. I went to the beach and I had an ice cream.

contrast: explain differences between things

deduction: working out meaning from evidence to find an overall meaning. For example, a pupil is late to school and has forgotten their books: deduction = they are not well organised.

delivery: the methods used when speaking aloud or presenting

demonstrative: adjectives such as 'this', 'these' and 'those' which answer the question 'which…?', e.g. Which books? These books. They are indicators

diary: daily account of events and actions

direct speech: the words they actually spoken, presented within inverted commas/ speech marks

explicit meaning: the clear and obvious meaning of a word/phrase/text

first person: when the story writer uses the 'I' form to speak directly as a character.

genre: a type of text. Fiction genres include science fiction, romance, adventure and horror

implicit meaning: the suggested meaning of a word/phrase/text which is not directly expressed

indirect or **reported speech:** words that sum up what was said, e.g. They said that they were pleased.

inference: an idea or conclusion that is worked out by using evidence. It is sometimes referred to as 'reading between the lines'

information texts: texts which provide factual details to help or explain things or processes

interview: a conversation in which the interviewer asks someone questions, e.g. when television journalists interview politicians or film stars about their work

journal: ongoing account of thoughts and feelings, possibly in response to events and actions. It does not have to be written every day.

metaphor: a more direct comparison than a simile, this says that something actually *is* something else, e.g. In winter, my dad is a bear in hibernation.

narrative: a series of connected events presented in the form of a story.
- can be fiction or non-fiction
- usually has at least one main character
- often includes thoughts and feelings of the main characters.

non-narrative: presents information in factual or statistical groups, not always in chronological order. Usually non-fiction, e.g. leaflet, brochure, encyclopedia, dictionary

noun: a person, place, thing or emotion, e.g. man; boat; love

personification: when an object is described as if it has human characteristics, e.g. The sun smiled down on us.

persuasive texts: texts which only present one point of view, e.g. adverts

playscript: the words and actions from a play written down for the actors to use

plot: the events that make up a story and how they relate to one another in pattern and order

plot obstacle: an event or incident in a story that presents a challenge or problem to the main character(s).

plot goal: the end to which the story is leading

point of view: a personal opinion or way of looking at something

preposition: a word that goes before a noun to describe its relationship to another thing or person, e.g. *on* the table, *by* my bed

purpose: the aim that the writer wants the text to achieve

quotation: words or phrases which are taken directly from a text to explain or support a point of view

review: a written report of a play, film, video game, CD, etc. which gives the writer's opinion offering a recommendation to others

rhetorical question: a question that is used to make people think (rather than to produce a specific answer)

rule of three: a useful pattern of three examples which makes the information or idea expressed memorable

scanning: using key words to find specific information in a text

semantic field: a set of words which are grouped around the same topic or meaning

setting: where and when a story happens

simile: imagery comparing two things using 'as' or 'like', e.g. My dad sleeps *like* a bear during hibernation.

simple sentences: contains one **subject** and one **verb**, e.g. The bell rang. The most basic sentence type

skimming: quickly understanding the main points in a text without reading every single word

stage direction: information provided by the writer of a play which tells the actor what to do or how to speak.

standard English: the form of the English language widely accepted as the usual correct form in any English-speaking country

standfirst: a brief, opening factual summary of news story

story arc: a continuing storyline that covers the main points in the plot

subject: the person or thing in a sentence that 'does' the action in a setence

summary: a text which provides a general overview or account of a situation or another text

Glossary

synonym: a word that is identical or close in meaning to another one, e.g. wet/damp

suspense: tense uncertainty about future events

tension: nervous excitement or anxiety

third person: when main characters are referred to as 'he' or 'she' by a narrator or writer.

tone: the attitude of the writer toward a subject (similar to the tone of voice that a speaker uses)

topic sentence: the sentence in a paragraph which shows the reader the main topic of the writing

verb: a word that expresses an action or a state of being, e.g. look, go, feel, think

verb phrase: uses an auxiliary verb attached to the main verb to help it change its tense, e.g. I could do; you should do

verb tenses: forms of verbs that express the time or condition in which an act takes place. In general terms, the past, present and future, e.g. I *looked*, I *look*, I *will look*

verse: a section of a poem divided into lines, often with rhyming words at the end of some lines

viewpoint: the perspective of a particular character in a story

Acknowledgments

We are grateful to the following for permission to reproduce copyright material:

Extracts from *Boy: Tales of Childhood* by Roald Dahl, published by Jonathan Cape Ltd and Penguin Books Ltd, pp.28, 86, copyright © Roald Dahl, 1984. Reproduced by permission of David Higham Associates Ltd and Farrar, Straus, and Giroux, LLC. All rights reserved; Extracts from *I am Malala: The Girl Who Stood Up for Education and Was Shot by the Taliban* by Malala Yousafzai with Christina Lamb, pp.11, 14–15, copyright © Salarzai Limited, 2013. Used by permission of Little, Brown and Company; An extract from *Red Dust Road* by Jackie Kay, Picador, p.37, copyright © Jackie Kay, 2010. Reproduced by permission of Macmillan; An extract from *Cider with Rosie* by Laurie Lee, published by Chatto & Windus, p.1, copyright © Laurie Lee, 1959. Reproduced by permission of The Random House Group Limited and Curtis Brown Group Ltd, London on behalf of The Beneficiaries of the Estate of Laurie Lee; An extract from *Faster than Lightning* by Usain Bolt, HarperSport, p.11, copyright © Usain Bolt, 2013. Reproduced by permission of HarperCollins Publishers Ltd; An extract from *Unbroken* by Lauren Hillenbrand, Fourth Estate, pp.147–148, copyright © Lauren Hillenbrand, 2010. Reproduced by permission of HarperCollins Publishers Ltd and Penguin Random House LLC; An extract from "Good deed giraffe man says he likes to makes others feel happy", *The Metro*, 15/11/2012, copyright © Solo Syndication, 2012; An extract from "Starbuck pay it forward chain nearly reaches 400 acts of kindness, then one person ruins it for everyone" by Louella-Mae Eleftheriou-Smith, *The Independent*, 22/08/2014, copyright © The Independent, 2014, www.independent.co.uk; An extract from *The children's Society Annual Report 2014*, p.3, copyright © The Children's society. Reproduced by permission; An extract adapted from *A Year of Doing Good: One Woman, One Year's Resolution, 365 Good Deeds* by Judith O'Reilly, Penguin Books, copyright © Judith O'Reilly, 2003. Reproduced by permission of Penguin Books Ltd and Conville & Walsh; An extract from 'Good Turns' by Lora Brinkman, http://girlscoutleader101.blogspot.co.uk. Reproduced with kind permission; An extract from "Target Employees Good Deed Goes Viral" by Jennifer Earl, CBS, 06/02/2015, www.cbsnews.com, copyright © 2015, CBS Broadcasting, Inc. Used by Permission; Extracts from 'Why Zoos Matter', Saint Louis Zoo, www.stlzoo.org, copyright © Saint Louis Zoo. Reproduced with permission; Extracts from *Penguin Beach* and *Gorilla Kingdom*, Zoological Society of London, www.zsl.org. Reproduced with permission of ZSL; An extract from "A Face like a surprised coconut", *Essential Articles 2014*, Volume 16, pp.11–13, www.completeissues.co.uk. Complete Issues copyright © carelpress.co.uk, with thanks to The Orangutan Foundation, www.orangutan.org.uk; An extract from "Look into the eyes of a caged tiger and you will see the zombie victim of 'zoochosis'" by Damien Aspinall, *The Mail on Sunday*, 30/07/2008, copyright © Solo Syndication, 2008; An extract from 'Endangered species' by Margaret Mittlebach, KIDS DISCOVER Spotlight, www.kidsdiscover.com. Reproduced with permission; Extracts from *Game of Thrones: Book One of A Song Of Ice and Fire* by George R. R. Martin, Harper Voyager, pp.7–9, copyright © George R. R. Martin 1996. Reproduced by permission of HarperCollins Publishers Ltd and Bantam Books, an imprint of Random House, a division of Random House LLC. All rights reserved; An extract from *Bloodtide* by Melvin Burgess, Andersen Press, p.75, copyright © 2013. Reproduced by permission of Andersen Press Ltd; An extract from *The First Men in the Moon* by H. G. Wells, pp.67–68. Reproduced by permission of United Agents LLP on behalf of The Literary Executors of the Estate of H. G. Wells; Extracts adapted from *Eragon* by Christopher Paolini, published by Corgi Children's, pp.6, 10, and *Eldest* by Christopher Paolini, published by Corgi Children's, pp.98–99. Reproduced by permission of The Random House Group and Penguin Random House LLC; An extract from *Elidor* by Alan Garner, pp.30–32, copyright © Alan Garner, 1965. Reproduced by permission of HarperCollins Publishers Ltd and Curtis Brown Group Ltd, London; Extracts from *Jimmy Coates: Revenge* by Joe Craig, pp.117–118, 236–237, copyright © Joe Craig, 2007. Reproduced by permission of HarperCollins Publishers Ltd and Curtis Brown Group Ltd, London; An extract from *Beauty and the Beast* by Laurence Boswell, Nick Hern Books, p.35, copyright © 1996. Reproduced by permission of Nick Hern Books; The poem 'The Magic Seeds' by James Reeves published in *Complete Poems for Children*, Faber Finds, 2009, p.118, copyright © The Estate of James Reeves. Reproduced by permission of Artist's Estate via Laura Cecil Literary Agency; and an extract from *Ingo* by Helen Dunmore, pp.105–107, copyright © Helen Dunmore, 2005. Reproduced by permission of HarperCollins Publishers Ltd, A P Watt at United Agents on behalf of Helen Dunmore, and HarperCollins Publishers.

Acknowledgments

The publishers would like to thank the following for permission to reproduce pictures in these pages:

Cover: Shutterstock/outdoorsman; p7: Dariush M/Shutterstock.com; p9, top: John MacDougall/AFP/ GettyImages, bottom: Jacek Chabraszewski/Shutterstock.com; p10: Frank Herholdt/Getty Images; p11: Adrian T Jones/Shutterstock.com; p12: Asianet-Pakistan/Shutterstock.com; p13: © F1online digitale Bildagentur GmbH/Alamy Stock Photo; p14: Victor Tyakht/Shutterstock.com; p15: Diego Cervo/ Shutterstock.com; p16, left: Yongyut Kumsri/Shutterstock.com, right: Aaron Amat/Shutterstock. com; p17: Ekaterina Pokrovsky/Shutterstock.com; p18–19: Matthew Dixon/Shutterstock.com; p20: davemhuntphotography/Shutterstock.com; p21: schankz/Shutterstock.com; p22: Michael Steele/Getty Images; p24: Frank Scherschel/The LIFE Picture Collection/Getty Images; p27: mubus7/Shutterstock. com; p29: JGI/Jamie Grill/Getty Images; p30: marekuliasz/Shutterstock.com; p31: exopixel/Shutterstock. com; p33: John Sartin/Shutterstock.com; p34: KidStock/Getty Images; p35: olio/iStockphoto.com; p36: weedezign/Shutterstock.com; p39, top: Ewelina Wachala/Shutterstock.com, bottom: Monkey Business Images/Shutterstock.com; p42: Lobsterclaws/Getty Images; p43: Illych/Shutterstock.com; p45: Maxx- Studio/Shutterstock.com; p47: Air Images/Shutterstock.com; p48: Caiaimage/Robert Daly/Getty Images; p50: michaeljung/Shutterstock.com; p52: michaeljung/Shutterstock.com; p54: Religious Images/UIG/Getty Images; p56: Piotr Wawrzyniuk/Shutterstock.com; p57: © Vincent DeWitt/Alamy Stock Photo; p59: Edwin Butter/Shutterstock.com; p60: Edwin Butter/Shutterstock.com; p62: © Michael Kemp/Alamy Stock Photo; p64: Golf_chalermchai/Shutterstock.com; p66: dedek/Shutterstock.com; p67: Villiers Steyn/Shutterstock. com; p68: Zero Creatives/Getty Images; p70: Peter Wollinga/Shutterstock.com; p71: Sutanta Aditya/ Anadolu Agency/Getty Images; p73: Rich Carey/Shutterstock.com; p74: AzriSuratmin/Shutterstock.com; p75: Dmitri Gomon/Shutterstock.com; p76: ppl/Shutterstock.com; p77: YanLev/Shutterstock.com; p79: MP cz/Shutterstock.com; p81: Eduard Kyslynskyy/Shutterstock.com; p82: Yaromir/Shutterstock.com; p84: CroMary/Shutterstock.com; p85: worradirek/Shutterstock.com; p86: Damson/Shutterstock.com; p90: © Eric Ghost/Alamy Stock Photo; p91: Dr. Morley Read/Shutterstock.com; p92: Pavel Vakhrushev/ Shutterstock.com; p94: Mike H/Shutterstock.com; p97: Chris Hill/Shutterstock.com; p98: Maks Narodenko/ Shutterstock.com; p99: dezi/Shutterstock.com; p101: Petrafler/Shutterstock.com; p102: urbanbuzz/ Shutterstock.com; p105: Attila Jandi/Shutterstock.com; p106: FotograFFF/Shutterstock.com; p108: Nagy Lehel/Shutterstock.com; p109: Claudio Divizia/Shutterstock.com; p111: diversepixel/Shutterstock. com; p113: © Antony Nettle/Alamy Stock Photo; p114: leungchopan/Shutterstock.com; p116: Kanea/ Shutterstock.com; p117: Andrey Yurlov/Shutterstock.com; p119: Ricardo Reitmeyer/Shutterstock.com; p120: qvist/Shutterstock.com; p121: © ATStockFoto/Alamy Stock Photo; p122: Rolf E. Staerk/Shutterstock. com; p124: Ollyy/Shutterstock.com; p126: andreiuc88/Shutterstock.com; p127: © Agencja Fotograficzna Caro/Alamy Stock Photo; p128: © Moviestore collection Ltd/Alamy Stock Photo; p129: Helen Hotson/ Shutterstock.com; p131: F. Jimenez Meca/Shutterstock.com; p133: Matt Gibson/Shutterstock.com; p134: Dmitry Elagin/Shutterstock.com; p135: Tatiana Popova/Shutterstock.com; p136: Amy Johansson/ Shutterstock.com; p137: Vitalii Hulai/Shutterstock.com; p138, top: Solid Web Designs Ltd/Shutterstock. com, bottom: thepiwko/Shutterstock.com; p141: Christian Bertrand/Shutterstock.com; p142: Brian A Jackson/Shutterstock.com; p144: sbko/Shutterstock.com; p146: Sabphoto/Shutterstock.com; p147, top: Valery Sidelnykov/Shutterstock.com, bottom: AVN Photo Lab/Shutterstock.com; p149: Africa Studio/ Shutterstock.com; p151: Colin Willoughby/ArenaPAL/Topfoto; p153: Peter Bischoff/Getty Images; p154: Cheryl Hill/Shutterstock.com; p157: Colin Willoughby/ArenaPAL/Topfoto; p158: Courtesy E/REX Shutterstock; p159: Chris Humphries/Shutterstock.com; p160: © Gino's Premium Images/Alamy Stock Photo; p162: Margot Petrowski/Shutterstock.com; p163: BGSmith/Shutterstock.com; p164: Blackday/ Shutterstock.com; p167: © Collection of the Earl of Pembroke, Wilton House, Wilts/Bridgeman Images; p168: Singkham/Shutterstock.com; p169: © Tony Lilley/Alamy Stock Photo; p171: lculig/Shutterstock. com; p174: World History Archive/UIG/Getty images; p175: Kipling Brock/Shutterstock.com; p176: © Bruce Rasner/Rotman/Naturepl.com; p178: DmitriMaruta/Shutterstock.com; p179: Andrea Izzotti/ Shutterstock.com; p180: Steven Maltby/Shutterstock.com; p181: bierchen/Shutterstock.com; p184: Alex Pix/Shutterstock.com; p188: Michael Baynes/Shutterstock.com; p191: Willyam Bradberry/Shutterstock. com; p192: MarcelClemens/Shutterstock.com; p193: Bildagentur Zoonar GmbH/Shutterstock.com; p195: Luiz Felipe V. Puntel/Shutterstock.com